WIDE OPEN TO TERRORISM

by Tony Lesce

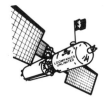

Loompanics Unlimited
Port Townsend, Washington

Wide Open To Terrorism

Published by:
Loompanics Unlimited
PO Box 1197
Port Townsend, WA 98368
Loompanics Unlimited is a division of Loompanics Enterprises, Inc.

Cover design by Dan Wend

ISBN 1-55950-138-3
Library of Congress Card Catalog 95-81596

Contents

Introduction

The 1995 bombing of the Alfred P. Murrah Federal Building in Oklahoma City was only a focal point for media hysteria over events that have a long history. At the moment, it's trendy to blame right-wing politics and organizations for terrorist violence, but 25 years ago the reality was quite different. At the time, left-wing organizations such as the Weather Underground and various racial groups were detonating bombs in public places such as the University of Michigan campus at Ann Arbor.

The Alfred P. Murrah Federal Building is a mute witness to the destructive power of modern day domestic terrorism. (Photo by Chuck Shiver.)

Actually, we don't have to look that far back. The World Trade Center bombing in 1993 demonstrated clearly how vulnerability to almost any sort of terrorism, including foreign political terrorism, is normal in our country. A few years before, the Pan American Boeing 747 that was downed by a bomb over Lockerbie, Scotland, might just as well have crashed on New York City.

Other countries are experiencing unprecedented acts of terrorism, as well, the sort of acts that could well happen in the United States. The radical group that released the nerve gas Sarin in the Tokyo subway in 1995 might have chosen New York City. In fact, one New York resident expressed surprise that they hadn't.

Terrorism is an uncomfortable fact of 20th century life. One supremely important reason for this is that the government cannot protect its citizens against terrorism. It's possible to protect against a foreign army and foreign invasion. It's possible to protect against some of the effects of natural disasters. It's even possible to protect citizens against some economic threats, such as loss of income. However, no government can protect its citizens against domestic or foreign terrorists, who strike without warning and in places the country is most vulnerable.

This is because "the terrorist makes the rules," striking at the time and place he chooses.[1] As we'll see, it's not possible to guard all vulnerable points all of the time, and the terrorist simply selects accessible targets. The terrorist is very flexible, responding to security measures used to defend against him. The terrorist switches tactics and targets, attacking those which remain unprotected.[2]

An open society such as ours is more vulnerable to terrorism than a closed society that uses media control, internal passports, residency permits, and ubiquitous police surveillance. However, one way that terrorists "win" is by forcing an open society to adopt police-state measures for protection against them. We've already seen security checkpoints, identification cards and the like in America.

This is a pessimistic book, because the picture is becoming worse. Terrorism isn't merely a foreign influence. It's clear that terrorism is as "American as apple pie," despite the media portraying it as a foreign import, and we're bound to see more of it in the future, even if foreign influences were to disappear miraculously. This is why most incidents and movements described in this book are American. Foreign incidents mentioned, such as suicide bombings, are to illustrate events that haven't yet happened here, but may soon.

The future will bring more terrorism here because of growing imbalances in our society. The United States' racial problems, far from being solved, are getting worse. As population grows and economic conditions worsen for those at the bottom, the pressure for violence will increase. Countermeasures will slowly lead to a garrison state, roughly like those in Israel and South Africa.

What This Book Will Do For You

This book is written for three types of Americans. First, it's for law enforcement and security professionals who have to cope with a variety of threats to public safety. Secondly, it's for legislators, to provide the sort of hard-edged information they need to make realistic legislative decisions regarding terrorism. Finally, it's for the citizen and taxpayer, who pays the price for all of this, whether he or she wants to or not, and suffers the severest consequences. The government takes steps to protect its leaders and main supporters, but the unfortunate fact is that the government writes off the average citizen as expendable. Court decisions have affirmed that the police have no duty to protect any specific individual. The only choice left for Joe Six-pack is to protect himself.

This book will provide background information on terrorists: how they think, how they work, and what they try to achieve. The practical information presented here will allow you to make realistic decisions regarding dangers you might face from terrorists, and how best to protect yourself against these threats.

This book will cover several aspects of terrorism and countermeasures in an unemotional and sober manner. We'll examine our country's vulnerabilities, the prospects for improvement, and various protective measures available. We'll discuss specific anti-terrorist measures that are possible today, and their suitability for the American scene. We'll also balance protective techniques and tactics against their public impact, to try to evaluate need versus price.

At the same time, this book will not provide the potential terrorist or bomb-maker with any recipes for explosives, poison gas, or other noxious substances. There are no diagrams of how to make bombs, boobytraps, or other destructive devices. With the plethora of sources for this sort of information, there's no need to add another.

Research quickly showed that it's possible to compile an encyclopedia on terrorism because so much material is available. Producing a book that would not quickly tire the reader with a profusion of facts required ruthless pruning. I hope this book will be complete enough to be practical without being too time consuming to read.

Compiling this book required a lot of research and interviews in both the private and public security sectors. One very helpful person who shared his expertise was Louis R. Lehner, security consultant and Certified Protection Professional.

The author also owes thanks to many who allowed him to pick their brains, but for various reasons, declined to be identified and credited. Thanks to Al, Bernie, Dave, Joe, John, Joyce, Sharon, Tom, and many others. They provided valuable and timely information, and any mistakes and mis-interpretations are my own.

Notes:

1. *Terrorism*, Holms, John Pynchon, and Burke, Tom, NY, Pinnacle Books, 1994, p. 215.
2. Jenkins, Brian, "International Terrorism: The Other World War," *International Terrorism*, Kegley, Charles W., Editor, NY, St. Martin's Press, 1990, p. 37.

Chapter One
The Nature of Terrorism

The term "terrorism" and its use often depends on viewpoint. One man's "terrorist" is another's "freedom fighter." To a dictator, rebels are "terrorists," but to the dictator's opponents and victims, they're "freedom fighters."

The same people can be both "terrorists" and be denouncing terrorists at different times. In one of the major ironies of human history, certain Israeli politicians who have been complaining about the rebellions and terrorist acts in their occupied territories were themselves terrorists during their early years. Itzak Shamir was a member of the Stern Gang, a terrorist organization, that attacked British officials and blew up British installations in Palestine during the years before Israel became a nation. Menachem Begin, who later became prime minister, was in the Irgun, another terrorist group that attacked Arab villages, blew up British headquarters, and carried out assassinations of people they didn't like. Ironically, Begin won the Nobel Peace Prize in 1978.

There are many ways to define terrorism, none of which are ideal. Some experts have laid out meticulous discussions of every minor point about terrorism, covering revolutionaries, conceptualizing political terrorism, political underpinnings, strategy of terrorism, and even the "multi-dimensional challenge of terrorism."[1] Some treatments are legalistic, others are philosophical, and all are simplistic.

A simple definition of terrorism is "a real or threatened act of violence, perpetrated by an organized group for political ends." This is the substance of the way the FBI defines terrorism, a widely accepted, seemingly common-sense definition, but it excludes many acts which are equally destructive, because they were committed for profit or non-political ends. The gasoline bombing of an after-hours club in the Bronx, New York, in April, 1990, killed 87 people, but doesn't fall into the "terrorism" category because it wasn't political. It was merely the spiteful action of one deranged individual, but until 1995, it was the largest mass murder in American history.

In 1964, members of civil-rights groups threatened to hold "stall-ins," blocking main roads, parkways, and expressways around the New York World's Fair. The technique was to run old cars with almost empty tanks onto the major arteries until they were out of fuel, and let them stall to obstruct traffic. The intent was to shut down the World's Fair by creating a massive traffic jam. This would not have fit into the category of "violence," because there would have been no personal injuries, loss of life, or property destruction; only a number of purposely disabled vehicles blocking traffic.

More recently, gunfire directed against Greyhound buses was allegedly the result of a labor dispute in 1990. This put it outside the conventional definition of "terrorism." There were attacks on buses in nine states, and in one instance, flying glass fragments injured seven passengers. In some areas, Greyhound buses received police protection.[2]

Although not fitting an official definition of terrorism, some tactics used by either side during a labor dispute are violent, and surely of a terrorist nature. There have been physical assaults on groups and individuals, as management has used "goon squads" of strikebreakers against striking employees. Strikers have also damaged their employer's property, which at times is very vulnerable. During a bakery strike in Phoenix, Arizona, over 20 years ago, strikers ambushed and vandalized bakery delivery trucks, and destroyed displays of baked goods in supermarkets. During a newspaper strike, union members destroyed newspaper vending machines. Another tactic was the firebombing of newspaper delivery trucks during a 1990 strike at the *New York Daily News.*[3]

Some product tampering doesn't fit the official definition, either. One man put sulfuric acid in his young son's baby food in the 1980s, so that he could sue the manufacturer, but this is also outside the narrow definition of "terrorism." In Britain, the 1984 threatened tampering of Mars Bars was politically motivated, as the threats came from the Animal Liberation Front, an animal-rights group. The 1982 Tylenol poisonings were not political acts. They did, however, cause terror in the sense that supermarket customers didn't know if the next item they bought might contain noxious substances.

Repeated acts of sabotage in the 1980s, against a Moslem mosque and cultural center adjacent to Arizona State University in Tempe, Arizona, also may not fit strictly into the FBI's definition because the perpetrators were never caught. This makes it impossible to establish that they were affiliated with a particular religious or political group.

At the time of the Gulf War, the FBI stated that only five "confirmed" terrorist incidents had ever occurred in the United States.[4] This figure is laughable, and shows how official definitions can be so convoluted as to make them worthless.

The U.S. State Department doesn't do any better. Its 1989 report showed a 40 percent drop in terrorist attacks from 1988, mainly because 1989 did not see a mass killing of the sort that happened over Lockerbie. Another problem with the State Department's figures is that the bean-counters tally incidents only when they involve citizens of "more than one country."[5]

Official definitions also ignore the increasing numbers of individual terrorists, some of whom aren't even affiliated with a sponsoring organization. John Salvi, who shot up several abortion clinics in 1994, was one example. Other lone individuals include the "disgruntled" employee going back to the office and killing his boss and other employees to make a point, or an environmentalist hammering spikes into trees which result in injury to the lumberjacks who attempt to cut down the trees.[6]

We also hear of "state-sponsored" terrorism. When someone uses this term, it usually applies to a cause or group he dislikes. Nations of various ideologies and purposes sponsor resistance movements in other countries, and such movements are usually violent. Some nations also send secret agents abroad to commit assassinations and other terrorist acts. When the Israelis sent out hit teams to shoot and bomb the Arab leaders responsible for the Munich massacre, they used methods similar to those sometimes used by Arab terrorists.

It's better to adopt a loose and practical definition of "terrorism." First, terrorism is a problem solving technique. A group of people, or an individual, have a grievance against a social system, social agency, or even an employer or former employer. Unable or unwilling to solve the problem through legal channels, they adopt violence to cope with their problem.

Sometimes the problem is an oppressive government, unresponsive to its citizens because it only serves the needs of the rulers. Another problem may be a movement or practice, such as abortion or animal experimentation, that conflicts with the terrorists' ethical or religious standards, although legal under the laws then in force. Getting no help from the "system," the terrorists feel they have to adopt extralegal means to attain their goal.

Another example is in the area of minority relations. The United States has had a race relations problem since its inception, because of slavery, and it's become worse over the years. Immigration has created "cultural diversity," which isn't the unmixed blessing the politically correct types claim it to be. As the minority population has increased and diversified, more frictions have developed. Ghetto riots of the 1960s often began after an incident involving Caucasian police officers and minority citizens. Acquiring territories has produced other ethnic terrorists, such as those in the Puerto Rican separatist movement. Today, young minority members are potential recruits for various "liberation fronts" and other terrorist groups which commit criminal acts to obtain funding for their organizations. At times, the result is a riot, such as those in the 1960s, and the one that took place in Los Angeles in 1992 after the first Rodney King trial.[7]

Contrary to some opinions, terrorists are not necessarily mentally disturbed. One psychiatrist who actually examined some terrorists, instead of merely theorizing, found that they were both intelligent and humorous, and showed no symptoms of mental disorders.[8] It's very safe to say that the majority of terrorists are perfectly sane. The reason is simple. An individual with peculiar ideas or delusions, such as the belief that government agents are shooting silver arrows through his brain, is unlikely to find sympathizers or collaborators. So is a person who wants to murder a former employer for having done him dirty. If anything, such a person's friends or associates are likely to try to discourage him from taking drastic action.

Terrorist groups are wary of accepting members who "openly seek excitement or danger."[9] Terrorism requires strict discipline of a different type than military discipline. Because terrorists often operate out of sight of the leadership, or even independently, they must have self-discipline. Reckless members endanger themselves and others, which is why "loose cannons" and "wannabes" are often detrimental to terrorist movements.

Some terrorist groups hold initiation rites, which involve some sort of criminal act. This isn't necessarily a "bridge burning act" to produce "common guilt," as some maintain.[10] This can also be a tactic to weed out police undercover agents.

There's no sharp dividing line in beliefs between terrorists and mainstream people. Some people have unconventional beliefs, while the beliefs of some terrorists are shared by many others. For example, many Americans today feel that the federal government has become too big, too expensive, and too oppressive. That doesn't make them terrorists, as most mainstream people make their feelings known at the ballot box, as they did in November, 1994.

The sharp dividing line is in behavior. Terrorists use threats and violence to attain their goals. To a terrorist, this is a shortcut solution, unlike time consuming moral persuasion, public demonstrations, arbitration, litigation, and other legal means.

Motives

Motives vary from lofty to self-serving. Within a single group, not all members are equally dedicated, and not all members wear an air of moral purity. As in any organization, terrorist groups consist of some altruistic and unselfish people, willing to risk their freedom and their lives for their ideals, and others with baser motives. There are hangers-on who affiliate with a group for personal profit.

Sometimes the motive is revenge. The Israeli hit teams that moved through Europe killing Arabs after the 1972 Olympic killing of Israeli athletes did so out of revenge.

The need for revenge is a very common human trait, and some individuals and groups are settling old scores while believing that they're improving society by killing their targets. Others do it for strictly personal reasons, without caring about the effect upon society.

Terrorist Morality

Both authorities and mainstream people are appalled by some terrorist tactics, such as killing and maiming innocent people. Government officials denounce terrorists as extremely immoral persons, but this is mostly propaganda.

There's a simple reason why terrorists adopt brutal and inhumane methods. They're merely following the same code of behavior that governments adhere to, a code based upon expediency, not morality. Governments do not behave the way their laws mandate private individuals to behave, and if a private individual behaved the way his government does, he'd be prosecuted.

During the 20th century, governments have authorized the bombing of cities by their armed forces, knowing that this would kill and injure innocent persons, including children. A government leader can cold-bloodedly order the use of weapons of mass destruction, considering the deaths of women and children "necessary losses," as long as they're not his own family.

This doesn't say much for the character of political leaders, and Henry Kissinger once stated that "Ninety percent of the politicians give a bad name to the other ten." However, politicians don't act in a vacuum, but with at least the tacit support of the people they rule. Many people also do not consider members of their armed forces as inhuman monsters, whatever weapons they use and however many innocent deaths they cause. In fact, members of the armed forces are fairly ordinary people doing a distasteful job because they consider it necessary. When many mainstream people accept and support political decisions resulting in many innocent deaths, it's not surprising that terrorists find it easier to justify killing innocents.

Practical Effects

If we decide to include acts because of their practical effects, instead of restricting the definition to one class of motives, it's clear that we're already heavily involved in a struggle against domestic terrorists. Disruption of an electrical network can cause economic losses, and even loss of life, whether performed by a deranged individual or a member of a political or religious fringe group. Sprinkling nails on a roadway can cause protracted traffic delays.

The outstanding feature of what we call "terrorism" is that a single act can have far reaching effects out of proportion to the act. Thus, a bombing or airline hijacking that results in diminished travel is definitely terrorism, because the terror produced by the act affects many people's behavior. The shooting of Archduke Franz Ferdinand in 1914 set off World War I. [11]

Many activist organizations, although supporting illegal acts such as blocking traffic and chaining themselves to furniture in public buildings, still do not propose violence or sabotage as official policy. Individual members may take more militant views and commit acts of sabotage. One woman, allied with an animal-rights group, planted a bomb at the U.S. Surgical Corporation in Norwalk, Connecticut, in November, 1988, trying to kill the company's chairman. The group disavowed her, and the bomb failed to explode.

Typically, officers of a militant organization will deny that the organization was involved with a terrorist act, although allowing that a sympathizer or individual member may have committed it. Unlike in Europe or the Middle East, where an organization will immediately claim credit for a violent act, the pattern in the United States is often denial. Immediately after the act, a spokesman for the organization most likely to have an interest will make a public statement piously denouncing violence, and claiming that the group was not involved. In reality, a particular organization may not have been responsible because the act was that of a freelancer. This is a very important point, because the knee-jerk reaction of some media people is to blame any organization they don't like, however tenuous the connection.

Special-Interest Groups

In this regard, it's also important to take with a grain of salt statistics put out by special-interest groups made up of members of minorities, those with offbeat political theories, and persons of unusual sexual orientations. There has been an increase in the numbers of "hate" incidents reported by these organizations in recent years, but these "bias crimes" statistics are often unfounded. "Intimidation" is one category of incident reported, but this can be anything from a stony silence, to a dirty look, to threats. It also may be totally imaginary.

These organizations report incidents to the FBI, although many are not federal crimes and only serve to swell the statistics. Most reports of incidents have no substance. Of the 8,918 "bias-related" crimes listed by the FBI in 1992, only 17 were race-related murders. Other serious crimes, such as rape, larceny and various thefts, arson, and murder, each "accounted for 1 percent or less of the total."[12]

When the Buddhist temple murders took place outside of Phoenix, Arizona, in 1991, the local leader of the Anti-Defamation League appeared on a radio show stating that this was a hate crime before police had any idea of the perpetrators. In the end, he turned out to have had no justification for his statement, as the mass murder was a cheap stickup that had gone wrong, committed by two thugs who themselves were minority members.

We also have to be careful with reports by Klanwatch, operating out of the Southern Poverty Law Center, Montgomery, Alabama. One of Klanwatch's reports dealt with white supremacist groups in the United States, and listed groups that sponsored or participated in rallies or marches, published newsletters or distributed literature, as well as those which engage in criminal activity. Holding marches or rallies is not illegal, and does not fit the definition of terrorism. Neither does publishing newsletters, a right protected by the Constitution.

Some of these groups may fit into the picture by being the legal, above-ground factions of a movement. As a practical and legal matter, it's not possible to prosecute someone for holding to an ideology, even if it's the same ideology as a violent terrorist group.

Terrorist Weapons

Terrorists have little difficulty obtaining the weapons they need. Domestic terrorists are ingenious, and make best use of commonly available tools and materials. Firearms are fairly easy to obtain, but other and more dangerous materials are even more commonly available.

Most domestic terrorists rarely use firearms, but when they need them, obtaining firearms is not much more difficult than buying tools at Sears. As we'll see, laws have no practical effects on obtaining firearms for illegal purposes.

American terrorists who need firearms often can afford to buy the best, such as this Heckler and Koch USP, in caliber .40 Smith & Wesson. (Photo by Tony Lesce.)

The safest way to obtain firearms without leaving a paper trail is to buy them privately in states which have no laws covering sales between private parties. Classified ads carry offers of firearms for sale, and some people sell them at garage sales.

A simple and secure way for terrorists to obtain guns is to purchase them through quasi-legal channels. This means ordering them from manufacturers or distributors, and having them shipped to a mail drop. This requires two items, an untraceable mail drop under an alias, and a forged Federal Firearms License, also known as an "FFL." One of the best-kept secrets is that it's remarkably easy to forge an FFL.

The reason is that to order a gun, it's required to send only a photocopy of the FFL to the distributor. Forgery requires only obtaining a legitimate FFL, obliterating the name and address with correction fluid and typing in the alias and the mail drop's address. A photocopy of the altered license is indistinguishable from a photocopy of a genuine FFL.

Another source is theft. Gun stores suffer occasional burglaries. So do government armories. A member of the Michigan National Guard testified before a congressional panel that "physical security on the base was a joke," explaining how he made off with whatever he wanted. [13]

This was not an isolated incident. In 1990, the Harrisburg, Pennsylvania, *Patriot-News* obtained government documents under the Freedom of Information Act, and concluded that the U.S. Army has hushed up many weapons thefts. The newspaper reported that since 1984, weapons stolen from military arsenals have been used in 349 bombings, which killed 13 people and injured 165. Weapons included firearms and explosives, mines, and rockets, which were sold to hate groups, drug dealers, contract killers and mercenaries. Customs officers even caught some people trying to smuggle some of these weapons out of the country. [14]

Later in 1990, a soldier and three others were arrested in Jacksonville, Florida, for stealing a "huge cache" of military weapons and explosives. The material came from several army posts, including Fort Bragg and Fort Campbell. [15]

Military thefts have happened in Canada, as well. In 1990, robbers killed an armory security guard and made off with 15 automatic rifles and six 9mm auto pistols. [16]

Firearms are serially numbered, which makes them easier to control with proper inventory procedures. Still, an officer in charge of the armory has several ways of covering up the disappearance of a pistol, rifle or machine gun. He can write a report that the gun was worn out or damaged beyond repair, and salvaged for parts. The paper trail ends with that report.

Ammunition, being an expendable item, is not serially numbered. Military units regularly issue ammunition for training, and it's easy to make off with a few boxes with nobody being the wiser. Theoretically, it's possible to account for every round, but in practice it's impossible.

An unusual way in which terrorist movements obtained weapons and explosives was by purloining supply dumps set up by the CIA during the 1950s. At the time, there was hysterical fear of the Soviet Army overrunning Europe, and CIA operatives set up ready-made resistance units, not necessarily with the cooperation or even knowledge of the European countries' governments. During the 1970s, when the need for these units appeared to have passed, local governments began recovering the weapons and supplies. Ten of the 139 stockpiles in Italy turned up empty, and their contents may have been used to replenish Italian terrorist supplies. Likewise in Belgium, there was a series of terrorist raids on supermarkets between 1983 and 1985, probably made possible by illicitly raiding underground supply dumps.[17]

A more recent example of U.S.-made weapons falling into the hands of terrorists took place after the end of the Afghanistan War. With thousands of Stinger anti-aircraft missiles still in Afghanistan, several delegations have offered to pay well for these weapons.[18]

The most risky way, in states with tight firearms laws, is obtaining them through the black market. The artificial shortage created by restrictive laws drives up firearms prices, thereby stimulating the black market. It's an ironic side effect of gun control legislation in this country that states and cities with the harshest gun control laws also have the highest crime rates, especially crimes committed with firearms. This is because criminals, not being law-abiding citizens, have no trouble obtaining weapons through illegal channels, where there's a strong financial incentive to supply them.

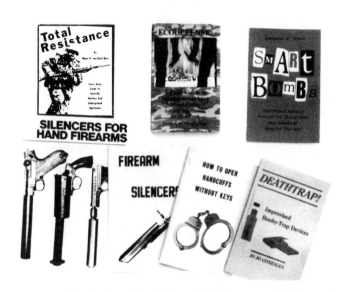

A variety of books describing improvised weapons and their use is readily available in retail stores and by mail-order. (Photo by Tony Lesce.)

However, illicit sources pose several risks. First, the weapons themselves may be "hot," in that they've been used in a crime. A criminal who fires shots during a crime will seek to get rid of the weapon as soon as possible, by discarding or selling it. A clever professional criminal, such as a contract killer, will strip down the weapon and drop the pieces in remote areas, where they're not likely to be recovered. A simple-minded or greedy street thug will try to recuperate some money by selling his weapon, and the buyer may be suspected of a crime he did not commit, if the police ever get their hands on that weapon.

Other personal weapons easily available are knives, garrotes, and impact weapons, such as saps and clubs. These are used less often than firearms, but offer the advantages of stealth and silence. The disadvantage is that they're "up close and personal," requiring proximity to the target. This can be a serious problem if the target has bodyguards, and some terrorists solve this problem by using a bomb, which blows up both the target and his party.

The biggest mass murders in American history did not involve firearms, a fact that apparently has not penetrated the consciousness of many legislators and media people. Gasoline and ammonium nitrate are much easier to obtain than firearms, because there's absolutely no control over their purchase. Compressed gases are available at any Wal-Mart, and some bombers use tanks of propane, butane or acetylene to enhance the power of their bombs.

The bomber who wants to use metal projectiles[19] in his bomb to produce injuries has many ready sources. Nuts, bolts, screws and nails are available in hardware stores, discount stores, home improvement centers and even supermarkets. We'll discuss bombs more thoroughly in the appropriate chapter.

Vehicles for transporting massive bombs are also readily available. Individuals responsible for both the World Trade Center and Oklahoma City bombings made the mistake of renting them, which allowed law enforcement officers to obtain descriptions. The World Trade Center bomber rented the van in his own name. Perhaps because he was a foreigner, he was unaware that by federal law all motor vehicles have a Vehicle Identification Number (VIN) stamped on various body parts. It's safe to assume that future bombers will learn from others' mistakes, and we can expect stolen vehicles to play a role in future bombings.

Exotic weapons, such as nerve gas and biological agents, are not only future possibilities, but are already here and in terrorist hands, as the Tokyo subway attack demonstrated.

Ingredients for these are also commonly available, but their manufacture takes considerable technical skill.

Special Terrorist Methods

Recruitment

Drawing new members into any underground group is fraught with danger. The recruit may be a loose cannon, irresponsible and likely to cause more trouble for the organization than he's worth. He may also be a police infiltrator, assigned to gather information. In some cases, the new member is an "agent-provocateur," who suggests that the group undertake a specific illegal act so that he may inform authorities, who then ambush and arrest the group.

Terrorists have developed ways to check out prospective members to ensure they're bona fides. One method is personal references; checking the applicant out with people known to them, to assure themselves that the person really is who he says he is, and not an undercover police officer. This background check is also a character check, and group members are on the alert for tell-tale signs of weakness, such as an arrest record. If the new member is facing criminal charges, he may be willing to work undercover for the police in exchange for having the charges reduced or dropped.

Another step in the process is initiation, which often takes the form of an illegal act. Knowing that police officers are not allowed to break the law to ingratiate themselves with those they're trying to infiltrate, the group will have the new member commit vandalism, arson, or a killing under carefully controlled conditions to prove himself to them.

Stalking

Stalking is often an individual crime, committed by an angry person against a former lover. One New Hampshire case involved a man stalking and harassing his former girlfriend by driving by her house and honking his horn, threatening her with an ominous arrangement of tarot cards, and slashing her tires.[20]

Stalking is also a tactic used by individual political attackers. Arthur Bremer, who shot presidential candidate George Wallace in 1972, had stalked Wallace and President Nixon for months before the shooting, attending political rallies while awaiting an opportunity to attack. Photographs of crowds showed Bremer's smiling face in several audiences.

Stalking is also a collective terrorist action, such as the coordinated stalking of abortionists and abortion clinic employees. Anti-abortion activists have used telephone threats, harassment, tire-slashings and other tactics to make life unpleasant for their targets, who become painfully aware that they're being closely watched by people who wish them harm.

Strangers On A Train

Alfred Hitchcock's 1951 motion picture, *Strangers On A Train*, dealt with two young men with motives for murder who agree to trade murders so that each may establish an alibi. This compelling theme has, in real life, inspired some terrorist groups to trade missions. Members of one group, unknown to police in the other group's territory, carry out the mission, while the other group reciprocates. The shootings at Israel's Lod Airport by members of a Japanese terrorist group were the result of a trade with Arabs.

A member of the Japanese Red Army, arrested in April, 1988, on the Jersey Turnpike, had with him pipe bombs and a map denoting targets in New York City. The plan apparently was to bomb targets in New York on the second anniversary of the air raid ordered by President Reagan on Libya in 1986.[21]

The Rise of Networks

It is a little-acknowledged fact that there have always been underground movements in this country, because some citizens have always had various reasons for evading government control and surveillance. Criminal and "street" gangs are obvious examples, but among less anti-social citizens, there have been underground railroads for former slaves, alcoholic beverage distribution networks, political and social activists, and others.

Experience had shown that the great weakness of centralized underground organizations is that police often unravel them by making an arrest, then obtaining information regarding other members from the suspect. Police repeat this process until they round up all or most participants. A well-organized group with a strong and well-defined chain of command is most vulnerable to discovery and prosecution.

The logical defensive measure for such organizations is breaking the membership up into "cells," or unaffiliated groups. This is what left-wing undergrounders of the 1970s called "affinity groups." Each group was unconnected with any of the others, and there was no central command structure. Arresting members of one group did not provide leads to other groups.

This practice dominates the illegal arm of the animal-rights movement. The Animal Liberation Front (ALF), for example, has no command structure, but publishes a training manual that states: "There is no formal membership. People become members by taking part in ALF actions, not by paying money and filling out forms."[22]

Earth First! also followed this principle. Until the leaders were arrested, after violating the security principles they advocated, they published *Ecodefense*, a manual for monkeywrenchers. The publishers took great care not to keep any records of who bought the book, and advised anyone corresponding with them not to put a real name or return address on their letters. Earth First! also made a point of not keeping copies of orders for their books, for fear that "plumbers" might burglarize their files.

The second edition of *Ecodefense* advocates keeping to small, separate groups of long-term friends who can be trusted. The authors point out that larger groups are more prone to infiltration, and that newcomers may well be dangerous crackpots or police informers.[23]

The book also contains a 63 page chapter on security, which covers target selection, recruitment, telephone security, camouflage, radio communication, pursuit and evasion, and other self-protective techniques. The emphasis is on keeping a low profile and being aware of the danger from informers. [24]

Keeping a low profile is an important security measure for the new terrorists. They do their best to blend into the crowd and avoid notice. Overt displays such as bumper stickers and political T-shirts advertise personal sympathies, and are sure to attract unwanted attention. Remaining apart from legal organizations advocating their point of view helps avoid being put on a police list. Avoiding open expression of opinions is another way the new terrorists shun calling attention to themselves. Keeping a low profile is very successful, because some terrorists have been able to gain employment at their target sites, thereby collecting valuable intelligence to help plan attacks.

Another point often ignored is that some police officers are members of terrorist movements. In the late 1970s in France, about 20 percent of the members of the Federation of European National Action, a fascist organization, were police officers.[25] There's no point in saying "It can't happen here," because closer to home, police officers have been members of the Ku Klux Klan and other terrorist groups. One reason why white supremacists got away with various terrorist actions in the South several decades ago was that the police "investigating" the crimes had been part of the action.

Drugs
Some terrorists use stimulants to enhance their fighting power. This practice dates from the ancient "Hashshashin," a corps of organized Middle Eastern contract killers who used hashish to stave off fear, pain and fatigue as they carried out

their attacks. The word "Hashshashin" became corrupted to "assassin" in later years.

Massive doses of drugs are harmful in the long run, of course, but this is unimportant to terrorists who don't expect to survive the attack. One of the terrorists who attacked the Rome Airport in 1986 was found to have amphetamines in his blood.[26]

Taking a combination of stimulants and depressants allows the terrorist to put out a greater physical effort than would be possible without drugs. Depressants also reduce fear, thereby enhancing the terrorist's fighting power. Some drugs, such as PCP, produce an insensitivity to pain, and those on PCP often show great resistance to blows and injuries that would incapacitate someone not on the drug.

Anti-terrorist teams are aware of this, and have concluded that it's often necessary to inflict massive injuries to stop a drug-induced terrorist. The firepower needed to stop such a person is usually enough to be lethal.

Terrorists Can Win

Today, it's politically correct to denounce terrorism, and to claim that terrorists have no legitimate aspirations. Some "experts" go so far as to state that any terrorist movement is doomed to failure because it's violent, and violence alienates sympathy. This is a simplistic view, and ignores the lessons of recent history.

The state of Israel began with terrorism against the British, who were the occupying power at the time, and against the Arabs, who had land the Israelis wanted. By calculated use of violence, the British were forced to withdraw, and Israel came into being in 1948.[27]

Another example was the Algerian National Liberation Front, which fused the diverse Moslem population of Algeria into a movement that eventually made it so uncomfortable for the French settlers and government that Algeria won its independence in 1962.[28]

Terrorists win local victories as well, an important point for those following a step-by-step strategy to defeat their enemy. One example took place in Tucson, Arizona, in 1988, where animal-rights activists forced a businessman to stop selling furs with a campaign of harassment and vandalism, which eventually convinced him that the cost of doing this sort of business was too high.

Some experts even mock terrorists. After the World Trade Center bombing, one compared the perpetrators to the Three Stooges, presumably because one had rented the truck in his own name.[29] This mockery disregards the severe damage they did, as well as their plans for other attacks which would have killed more people.

Some non-violent movements have been successful, such as Ghandi's effort in British India and the non-violent Martin Luther King faction of the civil-rights movement in the United States. In other places, at other times, violent movements have produced the desired results, as in Israel and Algeria.

Insurgents don't always win, especially if the government in power enjoys massive outside help. Filipino insurgents were suppressed with American help. Uruguay's Tupamaros failed and were devastated by government reaction. In the United States, the more violent factions of the black liberation movement suffered defeat because of poor strategy and tactics, failure to gain the confidence and support of the people, and a powerful and stable government. In Vietnam, however, the guerrillas and terrorists calling themselves the Viet Cong eventually succeeded.

Notes:

1. Kegley, Charles W., *International Terrorism*, NY, St. Martin's Press, 1990, pp. 1-96.

2. Castro, Janice, "Labor Draws An Empty Gun," *Time*, March 26, 1990, p. 56.
3. Cauchon, Dennis, and Frankel, Bruce, "Strike at N.Y. Daily News," *USA Today*, October 26, 1990, p. 2B.
4. Peterson, Karen S., "Question Gnaws: Will Terrorists Hit Here?" *USA Today*, January 19, 1991, p. 4D.
5. Kovsky, Steve, "Corporate Terrorism, A New Global Threat," *Management Review*, v79, n10, October, 1990, p. 39.
6. Lehner, Louis R., *Domestic Terrorism, Term Paper for Security Management 107*, July 7, 1992, p. 18.
7. Los Angeles Riots, *Time*, May 11, 1992, p. 18.
8. Crenshaw, Martha, "The Causes of Terrorism," Kegley, Charles W., Editor, *International Terrorism*, NY, St. Martin's Press, 1990, p. 120.
9. *Ibid.*, p. 121.
10. *Disaster and the Millennium*, Barkun, Michael, New Haven, CT, 1974, pp. 14-16.
11. *Disruptive Terrorism*, Santoro, Victor, Port Townsend, WA, Loompanics Unlimited, 1984, p. 13.
12. "Latest Hate-crime Trends Depend on the Source," *Law Enforcement News*, March 15, 1994, p. 5.
13. Glieck, Elizabeth, "Something Big Is Going To Happen," *Time*, vol. 145, no. 19, May 8, 1995, pp. 52.
14. "Paper: Army Hushed Up Weapons Thefts," Associated Press, October 15, 1990.
15. "G.I., 3 Others Held In Theft of Arms, Explosives," Associated Press, November 18, 1990.
16. "Guard at Armory Slain in Theft of Assault Rifles," Associated Press, December 20, 1990.
17. Nelan, Bruce W., "NATO's Secret Armies," *Time*, November 26, 1990, p. 44.
18. Castro, Janice, "Reaping What We Sowed," *Time*, May 11, 1992, p. 9.
19. Often mistakenly called "shrapnel," after the British officer who pioneered fragmenting artillery shells.

20. Moore, David, "Tarot Card Stalker: Police Say Stalker's Death Threat Was in the Cards," Associated Press, December 5, 1994.
21. "Bombs Across The Ocean?" *Time*, March 20, 1989, p. 26.
22. Lee, Edward L., "Violent Avengers," *Security Management*, v33 n12, December, 1989, p. 38.
23. Foreman, Dave, and Haywood, Bill, *Ecodefense: A Field Guide to Monkeywrenching*, Second Edition, Tucson, AZ, Ned Ludd Books, 1987, p. 15.
24. *Ibid.*, pp. 248-311.
25. *Terrorism*, Holms, John Pynchon, and Burke, Tom, NY, Pinnacle Books, 1994, pp. 53-54.
26. Magnuson, Ed, "Ten Minutes of Horror," *Time*, January 6, 1986.
27. Fromkin, David, "The Strategy of Terrorism," Kegley, Charles W., Editor, *International Terrorism*, NY, St. Martin's Press, 1990, pp. 56-57.
28. *Ibid.*, pp. 57-59.
29. Church, George J., "The Terror Within", *Time*, July 5, 1993, p. 22.

Chapter Two
History

The first American "terrorists" were the revolutionaries who broke free of British rule and founded the United States. The "Boston Tea Party" was considered a terrorist act by the authorities of the day. To the occupying power, the American patriots were traitors, and if the insurrection we call the "American Revolution" had failed, many would have ended up dangling from ropes.

Let's take a quick look at the course of terrorism in American history:

The new American government had to deal with an insurrection called the "Whiskey Rebellion," a coalition of farmers and distillers protesting liquor taxes. Washington had to send army troops to suppress this revolt. More revolts were to follow.

As slavery became a hot issue, some opponents took drastic measures in protest. John Brown, a prominent abolitionist, organized the assassinations of five pro-slavery citizens as deterrents. He and his band then raided the Harper's Ferry Arsenal in 1859 to capture weapons. A detachment of U.S. marines intervened, and John Brown stood trial for treason and ended up on the gallows. After the Civil War, the Ku Klux Klan used terrorism against Northern carpetbaggers.

After the turn of the century, "anarchists," most of whom were European immigrants, used bombs against establishment targets. In 1919, after a flurry of letter-bomb attacks, a bomb exploded in front of the U.S. Attorney General's house in Washington, DC. In 1920, a wagon bomb detonated in front of the House of Morgan on Wall Street in New York City, killing 35 people.

The 1960s saw an increase in American terrorism. While some civil-rights activists were non-violent, others urged that force was the only solution. Some made it a point to attack police officers on the grounds that the police were the white army of occupation. There was opposition to civil rights, especially in the South, which led to more violence.

The problem hasn't gone away. When a Hasidic Jewish driver accidentally ran down two African-American children in the Crown Heights section of Brooklyn in 1991, there was an immediate angry outcry against the Hasids. One sign read, "WE WANT THE JEWISH MURDERER ARRESTED NOW." Four days of rioting led to 163 arrests, 234 injuries, and one murder of a visiting Hasidic Jew from Australia.[1]

There are indications the problem may worsen in the near future. Myrlie Evers-Williams, new chairperson of the National Association for the Advancement of Colored People, recently announced in 1995: "Imagine the monstrous consequences if Newt (Gingrich) succeeds in making starvation public policy in a society where the poor are heavily armed."[2]

Organizations

Terrorist organizations come and go, which is why any comprehensive listing is futile. We'll discuss a few representative groups to provide the motivations and flavor of American terrorism.

The Black Liberation Army. This was a revolutionary group meting out "real justice" to the "domestic armed forces of racism and oppression," according to a letter sent by them to *The New York Times* in 1971, a few days after a submachine-gun attack against two New York City radio-car officers. Several days later, two African-American youths ambushed two more officers, Waverly Jones and Joseph Piagentini, in

Harlem, killing both. Jones was African-American, and Piagentini was white.[3]

These were not to be the only deadly attacks against police officers by members of the Black Liberation Army, an outgrowth of the Black Panthers. Early the next year, Greg Foster (African-American), and Rocco Laurie (white), were shot to death in an ambush on New York's Lower East Side.[4]

The Jewish Defense League began as a self-defense group in Brooklyn, New York, in response to rampant street crime in the area, but soon branched out to attacking people they didn't like. Harassment of Soviet and Arab diplomatic officials was one tactic. The JDL operated training camps in upper New York State to train its members in guerrilla tactics, assassination, and other types of terrorism. The organization has carried out terrorist strikes, mainly on American soil, although some of its members have emigrated to Israel.

The Ku Klux Klan began shortly after the Civil War as a reaction to carpetbaggers and other abuses under the Northern occupation. Basically, the KKK was a populist organization made up of white Protestant men who felt threatened. Its organizer, former Confederate General Nathan Bedford Forrest, disbanded the KKK in 1871 because of extreme actions taken by some of its members. There were several revivals, during the 1920s and again during the 1960s, when civil-rights agitation was at its height. A main concern is crime. The 1990 census showed that African-Americans comprise less than 13 percent of the population. FBI figures show they commit 60 percent of the murders. Forced school integration, which has resulted in lower standards, is another concern of Caucasians who join the Klan.

Puerto Rican Nationalists, under various organizational names, have pushed for independence for their island for decades. Some members have resorted to terrorism, including an attack against a U.S. president. Puerto Rican nationalists have instigated over 130 bombings in the United States. On November 1, 1950, Oscar Collazo and Griselio Torresola, armed with handguns, tried to assault Blair House, where President Truman was living during the renovation of the White House. During the shoot-out in front of Blair House, one White House policeman and Torresola were shot to death. Collazo and two other officers were wounded.

On January 21, 1981, Puerto Rican nationalists attacked the Puerto Rican Air National Guard Base in San Juan, destroying nine A-7 Corsair military aircraft.[5]

Street Gangs. Although organized for profit, street gangs are also terrorists because of the deaths and injuries they inflict. Gangs were responsible for 771 deaths in Los Angeles County in 1991, and for injuring over 5,000 persons.

Some street gangs, such as "skinheads," are racist and political. Their propensity for violence puts them into the "terrorist" category. Others are heavily involved in dealing illegal drugs, and regularly use violence to further their business interests. One practical result several years ago was that then-Attorney General Richard Thornburg began traveling in an armored limousine and on an FBI executive jet instead of commercial airliners.[6]

Symbionese Liberation Army. This was a revolutionary organization, also known as the "SLA," which originally promoted prison reform, containing both white and African-American members. The SLA soon began a program of violence, including the kidnapping of Patty Hearst, who converted to their cause during her captivity. Los Angeles police trapped and killed most of the SLA's members during an intense shoot-out in 1974. Some officers said after the battle that "SLA" now stood for "So Long, Assholes."

The Weather Underground was a 1969 outgrowth of the Students for a Democratic Society, a political action group with a definite left-wing slant. With about 500 terrorist acts to their credit, this group was a problem for law enforcement because of its propensity for extreme violence, including bank and armored car robberies. Three Weather Underground members died in an accidental detonation of explosives in their

Greenwich Village, NY, townhouse in 1970. The organization fell apart after 1981.

White Supremacists (and White Separatists) have formed several organizations, from the moribund KKK to the Aryan Nations, Christian Defense League, The Order, Arizona Patriots, and Covenant, Sword, and Arm of the Lord. They see themselves as beleaguered by African-Americans and their Jewish allies, which is why many of these groups are in the Western and Northwest states, which have relatively small black and Jewish populations. Various factions have committed murders and robberies, and some have been prosecuted for stockpiling illegal arms.

One group, the Silent Brotherhood, seeks to turn the Pacific Northwest into a white enclave, and was involved in an armored car robbery and the killing of a talk show host the group despised. Among other acts in the early 1980s, its members bombed a synagogue, robbed a Fred Meyer department store, and murdered a suspected informer.

Recent American Terrorism

The United States, despite a crime rate higher than most other Western nations, has suffered little from international terrorism during the 20th century. This is because terrorists are concerned with targets close to home. Middle Eastern terrorists have the Israelis in their back yard. The Irish Republican Army has British targets in Ulster and in England, just across the Irish Sea. British troops occupy their front yard.

We have become complacent, despite the active indigenous revolutionary movements since the "Weathermen" of the 1960s. Between various self-proclaimed ethnic revolutionaries and sundry political offshoots of the right-wing movement, several have resorted to violence. As we saw in the Oklahoma City bombing, it takes only a few individuals to inflict serious damage. Lately, there have been more signs of a renewal of domestic terrorism:

- Recently, in Central Arizona, members of a group called Earth First! were arrested by agents of the Federal Bureau of Investigation and charged with a 1988 attempt to sabotage an electric power network feeding the Palo Verde nuclear power station.

- Two people associated with Earth First! were arrested in 1990 after a bomb blast took place in their car. Although they denied knowledge of the bomb, a police spokesman stated that the two were arrested because officers felt that the evidence showed that they were transporting the device when it went off.

- In Santa Cruz County, California, sabotage of electrical power poles caused a blackout in an area serving 95,000 residents, during April 22 and 23, 1990. Investigators stated that they're not sure that the group which took credit for the sabotage, the "Earth Night Action Group," actually exists, but the damage was real.

- At Cornell University, a computer "virus" created by a graduate student, Robert T. Morris, Jr., got into the Internet/Arpanet system in 1988, and damaged information stored in thousands of computers. One estimate of the total cost involved in clearing the computers of the virus infection was $98 million.

- Some student terrorists of the 1960s have led long underground careers, and a few are still with us today. Linda Sue Evans began by protesting at the 1968 Chicago Democratic Convention, and branched out into an array of sabotage. She was sentenced in late 1990 in connection with a series of bombings dating from 1983 to 1985. This included a bombing at the U. S. Capitol.[7]

- On February 8, 1990, unknown attackers ambushed and killed Dr. Hyram Kitchen, dean of the University of Tennessee's veterinary school. The main suspects were animal-rights activists. A threat mailed to the school stated that one veterinary school dean per month would be killed for the next year. [8]

From these few instances, we can see that terrorists have not only increased their activities, but have adopted new methods for causing widespread harm. New technologies have made it easier to plan an attack, and easier to avoid detection and capture.

One such technological advance is a virtual reality program that provides views of the White House, distributed by Educorp, 7434 Trade Street, San Diego, CA 92121-2410. Previously, it had been necessary to rely on floor plans and photographs when planning an attack. This program provides a "virtual walk-through of both Air Force One and the White House." Another feature allows viewers to "experience what it's like to be surrounded by armed Secret Service officers." The price is forty dollars, a true bargain for the terrorist on a tight budget who wants to get the feel of his targeted premises.

The Anti-Abortion Movement

More recent terrorism has centered around abortion clinics, attempting to abolish them or to make it difficult for them to operate. There have been acts of vandalism, including bombings and fire-bombings, deadly attacks against abortion clinic personnel, and a variety of threats. This makes the anti-abortion movement a good case study of the evolution of peaceful protest into terrorism, and we'll explore its tactics and techniques in the next chapter.

Animal-Rights Organizations

A recently growing movement has been the "animal-rights" activists. Like opponents of abortion, many have used education and lobbying to promote their goals.

Other animal-rights activists harass anyone they see wearing furs. Calling them "animal killers" on the street, hurling paint on anyone wearing fur garments, these terrorists also vandalize stores that sell fur. [9]

Opposed to eating meat, using animals for furs, and medical experiments on animals, these activists have picketed and demonstrated, with some occasionally using harsher methods. There have been bombings, arson, destruction of records, spray-painting, and physical attacks on people.[10]

In 1985, members of the Animal Liberation Front (ALF) caused $500,000 worth of damage at a University of California laboratory. Raiders stole over 450 animals.[11]

ALF's 1987 raid at the University of California laboratory at Davis caused $3.5 million worth of damage. Animal-rights terrorists have vandalized over 90 laboratories between 1980-1990, and caused $10 million worth of damage.

In 1989, animal-rights activists raided the animal research laboratory at the University of Arizona, in Tucson. They stole 1,200 animals and set a fire, with total damage estimated at $100,000.[12]

A significant point regarding animal-rights terrorists is that they often infiltrate facilities they intend to attack. Having an employee on the inside provides valuable information regarding the facility's vulnerabilities, staff, and security systems.[13]

Even without an infiltrator, animal-rights terrorists can do enough damage to force the ending of a business they find objectionable. A Tucson furrier found that, since he'd opened his store in 1984, terrorists continuously vandalized and harassed him. They splashed paint on his walls, spread nails in his parking lot, and jammed his locks with glue. They also kept his phone ringing off the hook by placing fake ads in local newspapers, listing his phone number with offers of free manure, puppies, and baby clothes. Another tactic was to send subscription cards to magazines, and book and records clubs, filled in with his name and address. The precipitating event in the owner's decision to stop selling furs and to limit himself to shoes, handbags, and dresses was a bomb threat.[14]

Some animal-rights activists have taken to harassing hunters by spreading deer repellent in the area of a hunt, tearing down blinds and tree stands, and verbally harassing hunters in the field. Other tactics are playing tapes of wolf calls to repel animals, and even placing themselves between a hunter and his target. Some have stalked hunters until they were ready to shoot, then used air horns to drive away game. A few have physically attacked hunters. One harasser smeared bison blood on a hunter's face, while another struck a hunter repeatedly with a ski pole. In Tucson, Arizona, animal-rights terrorists threw a grenade into the U.S.D.A. Animal Damage Section's parking lot in 1990. Others have placed leg-hole traps to hurt bird hunters' dogs, and spread poisoned dog food in hunting areas. Placing nails and spikes on dirt roads used by hunters is another tactic.[15]

Another tactic has been to insult and verbally harass armed hunters, while a member of the group videotapes them. Any action by the hunters can then be displayed out of context, to promote the view that hunters are savages. There might even be a kamikaze element in this; the hope that a hunter would lose his temper and open fire.

Some organizations actively promote hunter harassment. Earth First! conducted a hunter sabotage workshop in Cameron, Montana, for anti-hunter activists, teaching them how to follow hunters and make enough noise to scare away game. Another technique suggested at the workshop is to spread chemicals or herbs to impair hunting dogs' sense of smell.[16]

Mohawk Warriors

A small-scale civil war erupted on the Akwesasne-St. Regis Mohawk Indian Reservation, spanning the U.S.-Canadian border, over the issue of gambling casinos. Proponents of gambling stated that the casinos supported about 600 jobs, while opponents stated that a by-product had been gun-running and drug smuggling. In 1989, 30 armed warriors blocked a highway, stopping a convoy of New York State Police investigating casinos. Gambling opponents torched a partly finished casino. In January, 1990, a Mohawk police station came under gunfire. A bombing of a police station took place in April. Armed men overran casino roadblocks and burned the vehicles of those manning them.[17]

Monkeywrenching

"Monkeywrenching" is a term coined by the Western writer Edward Abbey, author of the novel *The Monkey Wrench Gang*. This lighthearted piece depicts a band of ecologists who sabotage companies which are pillaging the environment, by disabling their machinery. This piece of fiction has inspired countless real-life counterparts.

Like the anti-abortion movement and many others, monkeywrenchers have both legal and illegal arms. An above-ground activist is Andy Kerr, operating in the Pacific Northwest, who uses litigation to make life difficult for loggers and sawmill operators. In turn, he has received death threats.[18]

A peculiarity of environmental activists, especially above-ground members, is their vulnerability to extralegal reprisals. One Florida woman was physically attacked in 1992 while fishing, by men who beat her and pushed a lighted cigar into her flesh. After cutting open her cheeks, they poured contaminated water on the wound, and warned her; "This is what you get for trying to make us lose our jobs."[19]

Vigilantes

Vigilantes are either individuals or ad hoc organized groups taking direct action to enforce the law, without support or endorsement by legitimate law enforcement agencies. At times, they serve a good purpose, such as when legitimate law enforcement is absent or unable to act against criminals. Unfortunately, some vigilantes determine that certain activities or persons are inherently criminal, and enforce their version of the law in their own way.

An example will illustrate this point. During recent years, there have been sporadic efforts to eliminate homeless people and drunks from our streets by poisoning them. The chief of police in a small town laced wine bottles with poison in 1990 in an extralegal effort to clean up his town's streets. Unknown persons left bottles of beer spiked with cyanide in the sleazy part of Phoenix to be picked up by drunks. One died from poisoning, and police suggested that two others may have died this way.[20]

In another case, vigilantes attacked a released sex offender to protect their community. New Jersey's newly enacted "Megan's Law," requiring disclosure of sex offenders' whereabouts, allows vigilantes to zero in on convicted sex offenders who move into their community. Two vigilantes broke into a sex offender's residence in 1995, but unfortunately captured and beat the wrong man.[21]

The Fallout of War

One effect of maintaining a large military establishment is that it produces a pool of people with military training, some of whom have combat experience. These veterans are trained in the special skills and talents of killing, and while most turn to civilian pursuits when they leave military service, the few who follow anti-social careers have a running start in the violent arts. While all are trained in firearms and marksmanship, a few have also had explosives and demolition training.

The United States has a solid history of terrorism, by various groups and under many names, and this trend is accelerating. Using harassment and violence to further personal and political ends has always been with us, and is now a well-established part of our culture.

Notes:

1. Allis, Sam, "An Eye For An Eye," *Time*, September 9, 1991, p. 20.
2. Francis, Samuel, "The Art of the Not-So-Subtle Threat," *Washington Times Weekly*, May 29-June 4, 1995, p. 30.

3. *Target Blue*, Daley, Robert, New York, Dell Books, 1974, pp. 89-101.
4. *Ibid.*, pp. 436-446.
5. Lehner, Louis R., *Domestic Terrorism, Term Paper for Security Management 107*, July 7, 1992, p. 11.
6. "Unlimited Mileage," *Time*, October 30, 1989, p. 54.
7. Pins, Kenneth, "Revolutionary Sentenced Today; Ex-Girl Scout Convicted in Bombings," *USA Today*, December 6, 1990, p. 2A.
8. *USA Today*, February 27, 1990, p. 4D.
9. "The Furor Over Wearing Furs," *Time*, December 18, 1989, p. 72.
10. Lee, Edward L., "Violent Avengers," *Security Management*, v33 n12, December, 1989, p. 38.
11. Burke, Robert R., and Hall, Gwendolyn F., "The Roar Over Animal Rights," *Security Management*, v34, n9, September, 1990, p. 132.
12. Lee, Edward L., "Violent Avengers," *Security Management*, v33 n12, December, 1989, p. 38.
13. Burke, Robert R., and Hall, Gwendolyn F., "The Roar Over Animal Rights," *Security Management*, v34, n9, September, 1990, p. 132.
14. Varn, Gene, "Beleaguered Furrier To Quit Business," *Arizona Republic*, January 20, 1988, p. B-1.
15. Conner, Beverly, and Leahy, John, "Hunter Harassment: Plaguing Our American Heritage," *Outdoor Life*, October, 1990, pp. 83-104.
16. "Earth First! Holds Sabotage Workshop," Associated Press, June 13, 1990.
17. Wood, Chris, "Gunfire and Gambling, Violence Explodes on a Mohawk Reserve," *Maclean's*, v103, n19, May 7, 1990, p. 22.
18. Seiderman, David, "Terrorist in A White Collar," *Time*, June 25, 1990, p. 60.
19. Toufexis, Anastasia, "Endangered Species," *Time*, April 27, 1992, p. 48.

20. Walsh, Jim, "Poisoned Beer Left in Public Kills Man," *Arizona Republic*, August 23, 1990, p. 1.
21. Weston, Donna Murphy, "Megan's Law: Two Charged With Attack In Sex Offender's Home," Associated Press, January 10, 1995.

Chapter Three
Case Study:
The Anti-Abortion Movement

A widely successful movement, involving a blend of moral persuasion, legislative/political action, and terrorism, is the anti-abortion movement. Although surveys have shown that a majority of Americans tolerate abortion, the anti-abortion activists comprise a large minority, enough to make their weight felt. The combination of political activism, peaceful demonstrations and overt terrorism has been successful, as it has for other causes and in other countries.

Abortion began as a noted growth industry, and today is big business. Between fees paid by clients and local, state and federal subsidies, the abortion industry collects many hundreds of millions of dollars. Planned Parenthood's annual budget, for example, is $500 million.

The anti-abortion movement began shortly after the Supreme Court's 1973 *Roe v Wade* decision legalized abortion in the United States. Opponents came in all types, from those writing an occasional letter to the editor to those willing to break the law. Several organizations sprang up, under such names as "Right to Life" and "Operation Rescue." Operation Rescue members appear to be more militant and willing to take risks than others, and some of them have been arrested for demonstrating in front of abortion clinics. There have also been activists, without formal affiliation to any organization, who have committed vandalism and other overt acts for their cause. This is what makes it hard to prosecute an organization for the actions of its unaffiliated sympathizers.

The anti-abortion movement, although fragmented, moved on several fronts, with a multi-pronged strategy of public demonstrations, harassment of abortionists and their allies, and vandalism and physical destruction of abortion facilities, while some extremists used gunfire against abortionists. As we'll see during this study, the rippling and overwhelming effect was to drive some abortionists out of business, and reduce the number of abortions performed in the United States.

Originally, anti-abortion protests consisted only of picketing and handing out literature. This had the effect of interfering with a lucrative business, and abortion clinic operators began seeking court injunctions and special laws against peaceful protesters. One example was the Federal Access to Clinic Entrances Act of 1994. This quickly became systematized by coordinated action against protesters, and evolved into a system of mass arrests.

The Conflict Deepens

Abortionists and their supporters quickly denounced right-to-life advocates as kooks and crazies. However, several surveys showed that religious right members are conservative and deeply religious people who act on their beliefs. Amitai Etzioni, president of the American Sociological Association, stated that he didn't believe that 40 million evangelicals have personality disorders.

Clyde Wilcox, Associate Professor of Government at Washington's Georgetown University, concluded that "The average Christian Right activist is a well-adjusted, well-informed individual." He added that "I don't think it's ever helpful to characterize your opponents as kooks."[1] Still, the insulting denunciations by abortion supporters continued, and have widened the gulf and lessened the chances of a peaceful reconciliation.

Early on, protesters' tactics had hardened in response to these personal attacks. What had begun as a non-violent struggle became more focused and the transition to violence was well under way. The trend towards violence has continued to this day. A public statement by Randall Terry, founder of Operation Rescue, revealed that the new program was to "shame them, humiliate them, embarrass them, disgrace them and expose them." The intent was to harass them until they quit performing abortions. Tactics involved putting up "Wanted" posters, cutting tires, pouring barbecue sauce on an abortionist's car, smashing windows, firing shots through windows, and picketing abortionists' homes.[2]

Protests continued, and abortion clinic operators developed close relationships with local police and courts to act against anyone interfering with their businesses. In Wichita, Kansas, for example, a court order resulted in the arrest of 94 peaceful anti-abortion demonstrators outside an abortion clinic in July, 1991. This was the clinic where the abortionist, Dr. George Tiller, would later be shot.[3]

Another example was the arrest of nearly 60 peaceful protesters outside a Birmingham, Alabama, abortion clinic in March, 1994. Ignoring police orders to keep moving, they knelt outside the clinic to pray.[4]

The Trend Toward Violence

After the Wichita arrests, protesters became even more aggressive. Some chained themselves inside abortion clinics. Others occupied clinics. Still others destroyed equipment.[5]

Fire bombs were favorite weapons, because anti-abortion terrorists soon realized that commonly available combustible materials are practically untraceable and very destructive. Two Kansas City, Missouri, abortion clinics were targets for fire-bomb attacks in December, 1994, but the effects were minimal. One bomb started a fire that caused about $300 worth of damage at Central Family Medicine. The attack against

Planned Parenthood may have been carried out by someone with little confidence, because two bombs were found at the front door. The wicks had apparently gone out, and neither bomb ignited.[6]

Anti-abortion activists have roamed the states, making careers of setting fires and bombs. Abortion clinics in Missoula and Helena, Montana, were fire-bombed in 1992 and 1993. One Montana abortionist found his home fire-bombed in October, 1993.[7]

One woman, Shelley Shannon, was charged with arson, dropping stink bombs in abortion clinics in four states, and setting fires at eight abortion clinics during 1992 and 1993. She had previously been convicted of the non-fatal shooting of a Wichita, Kansas, abortionist.[8]

Another woman used the same stink-bomb substance, butyric acid, against two abortion clinics in 1993. An elderly man pleaded guilty to hiring her to carry out the attacks.[9]

Stalking became another weapon in the anti-abortionists' arsenal. One man stalked, threatened and harassed an abortionist until convicted of violating several laws in 1995. Dr. Gerald Applegate stated that the stalker ran him off the road, sent him nasty letters, and demonstrated outside his home and office.[10] Court orders and convictions did not stop the anti-abortion movement.

Forcing Increased Security Expenditures

Immediately after shootings, abortion clinics far from the site became concerned for their security. Dr. Brian Finkel, a Phoenix abortionist, stated in 1995 that he wears a ballistic vest and carries a gun. Other clinic operators, unable to obtain permanent police patrols, have had to pay for their own security, spending money to hire additional security guards, install alarms and video cameras, and purchase metal detectors. For example, security consumes 20 percent of Planned Parenthood's budget.

Chilling the Atmosphere

An overt event produces a chilling effect. When an assailant fired three bullets from an AK-47 into the dining room of Dr. Garson Romalis, an abortionist in Vancouver, British Columbia in 1994, he produced a rippling reaction. Although only one of the bullets struck, wounding the doctor in the leg, police and other abortion supporters reacted with alarm. Romalis and his family came under police protection, as did other abortion clinics in Vancouver.[11]

In Pensacola, Florida, the chilling effect of the shooting of abortionists was even more severe in 1994. Two abortion rights leaders said that they intended to leave Pensacola because of "threats and harassment." Two doctors practicing as abortionists have been shot to death in Pensacola, and the two women intending to evacuate found their cars sabotaged.[12]

Fear and Attrition

Every attack against an abortion clinic has had a widespread effect, even far from where the attack took place. After the 1994 shootings at two abortion clinics in Massachusetts, fear rippled out and people employed at abortion clinics many miles away became apprehensive. Janie Bush, director of Dallas' Choice Foundation, stated that she feared walking out the door to be confronted by someone "with a shotgun."[13]

Norma McCorvey, the woman known as "Jane Roe" in the *Roe v Wade* case, expressed her fears of working at the abortion clinic in Dallas, Texas, where she was employed in 1994. McCorvey had previously been hit by eggs thrown from a pickup truck, and bullets were fired into her home.[14]

The next abortionist to work in the Pensacola Ladies Center clinic after the killing of the second doctor there did so anonymously, and an off-duty police officer drove him to work. But violence wasn't the only weapon employed by opponents of abortion. Another example of the chilling effect was that Dr. Steven Brigham quit his job after his records in New York and New Jersey were divulged by diligent anti-abortion activists who had investigated his past. Brigham's New York license was revoked in November, 1994, and there were complaints against him in New Jersey.[15]

An abortionist working at the Hillcrest Clinic in Norfolk, Virginia, where several bombings and one shooting have taken place, resigned in August, 1994, as a result of harassment.[16]

Four abortionists in Melbourne, Florida, stopped performing abortions in the early 1990s. Overall, there are fewer abortionists today than previously, and they're concentrated in major urban areas.

Almost no new abortion clinics are being built, tacit recognition that abortion has become a high-risk business. Between 1990 and 1994, about 200 abortion providers have stopped offering this service. The number of hospital residency training programs teaching abortion has dropped by half. 84 percent of counties in the United States have no abortion facilities. The Alan Guttmacher Institute revealed that abortions in 1992 were 1.5 million, the lowest since 1979.[17]

With fewer doctors performing abortions, some clinics are operating without any. One California clinic operator was charged with murder after a pregnant woman died during an attempted abortion at her clinic. Alicia Ruiz Hanna was convicted of second degree murder in December, 1994, in Los Angeles.[18]

A survey of abortion clinics by the Feminist Majority Foundation showed that there had been a slight increase in violence during the first seven months of 1994. Despite the new federal Freedom of Clinic Entrances Act, no arrests had yet occurred under the new law.[19]

Adding to this was the admission by Attorney General Janet Reno that the clinic in Brookline, Massachusetts where an anti-abortion activist shot two women in 1994, had no federal marshals guarding it because there were not enough available personnel. "Law enforcement does not have enough resources to deal with all threats," was Reno's statement.[20]

Some abortion advocates became hysterical. A few claimed that anyone who failed to speak out against the shootings was tacitly expressing approval of the violence. The mainstream media carried this viewpoint, taking the hysteria over the shooting of abortionists to greater heights, lashing out wildly at anyone taking an anti-abortion stance. One Vermont pro-abortion group went so far as to sue a printer for refusing to print their membership cards.[21]

Legal Action

There was particularly strong protest against late-term abortions, including "brain suction" procedures that involved partial delivery and suctioning out the unborn baby's brain before extraction. Florida Representative Charles T. Canaday sought a bill to outlaw these operations on the federal level 1995. Meanwhile, the Ohio legislature introduced a bill to outlaw such procedures in Ohio.[22]

Another hazard to strike abortion clinic operators was litigation, but from an unexpected source. The family of Dr. David Gunn is suing Pensacola Women's Medical Services for not adopting security measures after Gunn had received threats and his mailbox had been blown up.[23]

Abortions Decline

The costs of repairs, increased security, litigation, and probably increased salaries to employees because of the risks involved has greatly increased the costs of doing business for abortion clinics. Clinics that raised their prices cut off the bottom slice of the economic pie, losing some potential customers. Moral persuasion, and counseling and adoption services, may have convinced some pregnant women not to employ abortionists.

The net result is that abortions have declined in this country. The Centers for Disease Control stated that abortions dropped by 2.1 percent between 1991 and 1992.[24] Overall, the anti-abortion movement has been very successful, because of widespread moral support from mainstream Americans, and terrorism at selected points.

Notes:

1. Briggs, David, "Politics: Religious Right is Rational, Informed, Study Shows," Associated Press, April, 1995.
2. Hall, Mimi, "Abortion Foes Target Doctors; Goal is to Ruin Business," *USA Today*, February 5, 1992, p. 3A.
3. Usdansky, Margaret L., "Clinic Arrests Mount; Abortion Foes Target Wichita," *USA Today*, July 30, 1991, p. 3A.
4. Associated Press, March 29, 1994.
5. Hall, Mimi, "Abortion Foes Copy Wichita Protest," *USA Today*, September 16, 1991, p. 3A.
6. "Clinic-Bombing: Fire-bombs Placed at Two Abortion Clinics," Associated Press, December 15, 1994.
7. Associated Press, October 11, 1994.
8. Associated Press, October 24, 1994.
9. Associated Press, November 28, 1991.
10. "Anti-abortion Activist Convicted of Stalking Doctor," Associated Press, February 3, 1995.
11. Associated Press, November 8, 1994.
12. Associated Press, October 28, 1994.
13. Martinez, Jose A., "Clinic Shooting: Helicopters, Dogs, Videos: Search For Abortion Clinic Gunman Goes On," Associated Press, December 30, 1994.
14. "Abortion: 'Jane Roe' Fears Returning to Work at Dallas Clinic," Associated Press, January 3, 1995.

15. "Abortion Shooting-Hill: Doctor Who Replaced Slain Physician Leaves Clinic," Associated Press, December 21, 1994.
16. Taylor, Joe, "Clinic Shooting: Clinic Shot up by Gunman Has History of Protests, Violence," Associated Press, January 1, 1995.
17. Bayles, Fred, "Abortion Access Cut by Money, Doctor Training and Protests," Associated Press, April, 1995.
18. Allen, Jane E., "Abortion Death: Woman Dies at Abortion Clinic; Owner Charged With Murder," Associated Press, December 16, 1994.
19. "Abortion-Violence: Clinic Survey Shows Slight Increase in Anti-Abortion Violence," Associated Press, December 20, 1994.
20. Morris, David, "Clinic Shooting: Attorney General Says No Marshals Were Assigned to Clinic," Associated Press, December 30, 1994.
21. "Abortion: Supreme Court Rules Against Anti-Abortion Printer," Associated Press, January 3, 1995.
22. Price, Joyce, "Ohio Eyes Ban of Partial-birth Abortions," *Washington Times* (Weekly Edition), June 12-18, 1995.
23. Kaczor, Bill, "Abortion Shooting: Slain Doctor's Family Sues Clinic," Associated Press, February 22, 1995.
24. "Abortions-CDC: Reported Number of Abortions Declines," Associated Press, December 22, 1994.

Chapter Four
Our Appalling Vulnerabilities

In simpler times, when people were less crowded together and less interdependent, there were fewer opportunities for terrorism. Today, with many people totally dependent on others for food, power, transportation, and other necessities, there are many potential targets, enough for a moderately bright terrorist to cause tremendous destruction and/or disruption with little risk of apprehension.

Terrorism works in three ways:
1. Physical destruction and disruption.
2. The climate of fear created by terrorist acts, aided and abetted by audience-hungry media.
3. Extra costs for security measures brought on by terrorism.

Wide Open to Terrorism

We live in a delicately balanced society, vulnerable to widespread disruption and destruction. The United States, despite whatever surge of new "anti-terrorist" laws that may come about, is still wide-open to terrorism. This is a huge country, with many, many vulnerable points.

Primitive societies have few vulnerable points because of their simplicity. Our society is different. Systems are interdependent and centralized, but their vulnerabilities are widely dispersed. This is why our technological society, with its many interdependent systems, is vulnerable at many points, and attacks upon those systems have widespread effects. In a power grid or water supply system, every component must work properly for the system to function. The interdependence of our systems means that a failure in one system affects others.

A motor vehicle that knocks down a power line can black out many blocks. A mechanical or electrical accident can black out an entire section of the country. The Northeast grid, including New York City's power supply, fell victim to this in 1965 and again in 1975. An electrical blackout can paralyze transportation as well, because traffic lights, gasoline pumps and airport radars go out with the power failure. This is true of any advanced nation. A Japanese group cut railway communication cables in 34 locations on November 29, 1994. This stopped traffic on several major lines.[1]

When a subway system stops working because of a derailment, power failure or a labor strike, it has many far-reaching and rippling effects. Businesses are affected when employees and customers cannot reach them. A freeway accident in a metropolitan area has a similar effect, delaying employees on their way to work and delaying shipments. This has an inevitable impact on business.[2]

Another aspect of our vulnerability is the easy access to destructive devices and substances, and knowledge regarding their use, defying any legislative approach to suppressing terrorism. No gun control law could have prevented the Oklahoma City bombing, nor the gasoline bombing of the Bronx nightclub.

It's very hard to protect our many vulnerabilities because they're so numerous and so dispersed. Our society is pervaded by soft targets, giving terrorists almost unlimited opportunities. As we'll see, the rippling effects of terrorism expose many unexpected vulnerabilities.

Communications Soft Spots

The nation's communications networks are equally vulnerable because they depend on an array of wires, satellites, relay stations and central switching facilities, most of which are accessible to terrorists. Microwave-relay stations are typically in remote areas, and all have well-graded access roads for maintenance. They're typically unguarded, and "security" at these sites is usually only a chain-link fence and perhaps an alarm. Even with locked gates and alarms, it's necessary for police or private guards to respond, and they're not likely to arrive in time.

While it's too fanciful to imagine that terrorists would be able to destroy satellites, all communication satellites have ground stations, which are much easier to reach.

Telephone company buildings, with their electronic switchboards, are extremely vulnerable, especially because they're not well-guarded. Security in telephone offices is limited to keeping unauthorized persons out and safeguarding telephone operators in the parking lot. As these buildings are usually in cities and towns, it's easy to park a truck bomb on the street outside without being noticed.

Radio and television stations maintain their studios in town, but transmitting masts are on the outskirts, preferably on high ground to maximize broadcast range. They're linked by landlines leased from the telephone company, which are accessible through manholes dotting the route. Transmitters are unmanned and guarded only by fences.[3]

Attacking communications links often requires only cutting a cable or placing an explosive charge inside or next to a building. If explosives are unavailable, gasoline will do because of the extreme vulnerability of electronic equipment to fire. A fire in one of New York City's telephone facilities in 1976 knocked out service for three weeks. Economic losses were in the millions.[4]

Terrorists rarely attack the mail, perhaps because it's so prosaic. The mail distribution system is extremely vulnerable, however, because mailboxes are everywhere. At the most basic level, a ghetto teenager in New York City can open a mailbox and flip his cigarette into it. This is a prank rather than a terrorist act, but it points the way to more extensive damage. A simple matchbook and cigarette firebomb can destroy the contents of a mailbox. A more sophisticated incendiary device, timed to go off after the carrier brings the mailbox's contents to the post office, can cause much more destruction. As collection hours are posted on every mailbox, no special inside information is necessary.[5]

In many areas, destroying a large amount of mail would seriously inconvenience many people. In a business district, mail destruction can deal a severe blow to companies because most business paperwork goes via U.S. Mail. Checks, purchase orders and other valuable documents are as flammable as personal letters, and a serious attack can paralyze a district's businesses for several days. The labor required to recover from massive mail destruction, including tracking and regenerating lost documents, causes further losses to the companies involved.

Voice mail is vulnerable to terrorism. At the very least, hackers using easily guessed passwords can gain access to a company's voice mail and retrieve sensitive information. Some of this information can be damaging if revealed to competitors, and other inside information can provide useful leads to circumvent the security system.

Altering existing messages, or planting false ones, can seriously disrupt a company's operations. An obvious prank is to plant an obscene greeting. This wouldn't do much damage, as company officials would quickly become aware of it and correct it. [6]

Transportation Vulnerabilities

Our transportation infrastructure is in poor shape and getting worse, making it more vulnerable to sabotage. It takes less effort to damage or destroy a structure or system already weakened by aging, decay, and wear and tear.

This is partly because of age and use, but lack of repairs and maintenance are major factors. When budgets are tight and citizens want lower taxes, a low-profile way to reduce the costs of government is to cut down on maintenance and replacement of roads, bridges and tunnels. This is why public works projects that took 20 percent of tax dollars in 1950 shrank to 7 percent by 1984.

Our decaying transportation systems are so vulnerable that in some cases they self-destruct. One example was the hole in a Chicago cable tunnel that flooded hundreds of basements, causing $500 million worth of damage.[7]

When a bridge is so rusted that a sign warns "Cars Only," it doesn't take much to complete its destruction. Jersey City's water mains are built of wood, vulnerable to both decay and sabotage. Some of the subway and elevated lines in New York and Chicago are a century old. All of these provide vulnerabilities for a terrorist who knows how to exploit them.

Subways and trains are extremely vulnerable because of the heavy traffic they carry and their ease of access. It's simply not practical to have metal detection and X-ray systems at every subway station, and terrorists know this. A gunman has easy access, and on December 7, 1993, Colin Ferguson shot six people to death and injured 19 others in a racist-motivated terrorist attack on a Long Island Railroad commuter train.[8]

Surface-train tracks are very vulnerable because they extend for many miles, and it's impossible to guard every foot. Removing a section of rail will stop all trains on that track until repair crews replace it. If the engineer fails to see that a section is missing, the train can easily derail. If a group of terrorists were determined to strike at the nation's rail system, removing sections of track at random over a wide area, this would cause a massive slowdown. Trains would have to run at much slower speeds to ensure that engineers would be able to stop in time to avoid being damaged.

In October, 1995, an attack by "Sons of Gestapo" derailed an Amtrak Sunset Unlimited train at a remote desert site 59 miles southwest of Phoenix, Arizona, killing one and injuring 78. The railroad warning system was bypassed by running electrical cord from a 19-foot track-rail section located at a bend in the track just before a trestle, to the adjoining rails. Then the rail joint bars connecting the ends of the track-rail section to the rest of the track were removed, along with 29 spikes. "If someone was intentionally setting out to derail an Amtrak train, this is how they would have done it," stated Thomas Downs, president and chairman of Amtrak.[9]

One type of sabotage that can bring every train on a line to a stop simultaneously is short-circuiting or cutting overhead wires in an electric rail line. Subways have third rails, and these are also vulnerable to sabotage, although access and escape is harder than for attacks on lines running in open country. As a practical point, it's easier to destroy a wire than a rail.[10]

Our road network is quite vulnerable to sabotage because of unlimited access. "Spiking" works on dirt roads where it's possible to place sharpened lengths of rebar.[11] Unknown saboteurs laid nails along the track for the Prescott (Arizona) 100 road race in 1991. They also moved markers and barriers in an unsuccessful effort to delay or stop the race.[12]

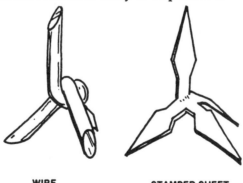

WIRE   **STAMPED SHEET**

Caltrops can be fabricated from wire or stamped, hardened steel. Either will puncture a tire and release the air, although the tire doesn't go flat instantly.

Sprinkling caltrops on a superhighway from a moving vehicle is a quick way to bring all traffic to a halt. Caltrops are available in army surplus stores, at gun shows, and can be improvised.[13]

Air Transport

Airports and airliners are also vulnerable, because there are so many of them and so many people have access to airports each day. There have been several instances of bombs exploding in American airports, such as at New York's LaGuardia Airport in 1965, because a favorite trick is to leave one in a luggage locker.

Several airliners have been destroyed during flight. Spectacular bombings such as the Pan Am 747 airliner over Lockerbie have far-reaching effects. One political effect is that it's become increasingly difficult to discount any bomb threat against an airliner.

To date, nobody has shot down an airliner over American territory, but this is a definite possibility. Overseas, members of the Zimbabwe African People's Union shot down two Rhodesian airliners with SAM-7 missiles in 1978 and 1979. Italian police searching an apartment under the flight path to Rome's airport found two such missiles, apparently intended for use against Israeli airliners.[14] In the United States, members of a Chicago street gang funded by Libya were arrested in 1985 while trying to purchase a missile to shoot down an airliner at Chicago's O'Hare International Airport.[15]

Attacks at airports and airline ticket offices have taken place in Europe, and there's no reason why they won't happen here. While airports have tight security on the flight concourses, terrorists have developed ways to overcome this. In 1986, two groups of terrorists delivered well-coordinated attacks against passengers in the vicinity of the El Al counter at both Rome's Leonardo da Vinci and Vienna's Schwechat Airports. The terrorists didn't bother to breach the security checkpoints, instead opening fire well away from the passenger gates. El Al's passengers were the obvious targets, but others got hit in the hail of bullets.[16]

Public Utilities

Our large and interconnected electrical power grid is especially vulnerable, because electrical power travels by wire and burying the grid to make it less accessible to terrorists or even weather damage is prohibitively expensive. This is why we experience occasional power outages.

Power stations are not heavily guarded, depending on a few civilian security guards whose main expertise lies in checking visitors against a list and watching to ensure that employees wear their security badges. Even nuclear power stations depend on security guards of uncertain competence, although some are organized into armed response groups in the style of police S.W.A.T. teams. The main thing such poorly trained guards have going for them is that an attack by armed terrorists is extremely unlikely. In any case, a person or group wishing to damage an electrical grid doesn't need to destroy a power station.

Threats can become very serious. After "vandalism" caused $200,000 damage to Pacific Gas & Electric in 1990, there was an increase in security. One company representative stated that they were considering the possibility of danger to company executives.[17]

The main problem is that our systems are heavily central-ized, but their vulnerabilities are decentralized, making them extremely difficult to protect. Like a railway network, an electrical grid covers a huge area, with hundreds or thousands of miles of high-tension lines passing through remote areas. Interrupting the power at any point will damage the system, blacking out a wide area. Earth First! activists suggest that removing the bolts anchoring a power pole is a way to ensure it will topple during the next storm or high wind.[18]

A 1990 report by the United States Office of Technology Assessment warned of the vulnerability of public utilities to both natural disasters and to sabotage. A small number of simultaneous terrorist attacks could knock out the power to a metropolitan area. Restoring partial electrical service usually takes only a matter of hours, but complete restoration could take months, depending on the severity of the damage.[19]

While water supplies make poor targets, flood control dams are excellent targets because they're mostly unsecured and unguarded. Destruction of a dam can cause large-scale loss of life and property damage, depending on the dam's size and location. Strangely, a typical flood control dam doesn't have any guards, or even a fence around it. This negligence provides an opportunity for a terrorist to place his explosives, set his timer, and be far away when the dam blows up.[20] Of course, once a dam is sabotaged, others will receive some security.

Hydroelectric plants are profitable targets. In 1976, when FBI agents raided a camp occupied by members of the Arizona Patriots, a survivalist group, they found maps of the Glen Canyon Dam at Page, Arizona, the Davis Dam (also in Arizona), and those for the Fort Thompson power substation in South Dakota.[21]

Fossil Fuels

Refineries and fuel storage tanks are difficult to protect because they're such huge targets. Pipelines are especially difficult to protect because of their length. The Alaska Pipeline, carrying petroleum from Alaska to the "lower 48" states, is 800 miles long, and most of it goes through sparsely populated areas where terrorists could commit sabotage and be gone before the effects became obvious. Delayed-action bombs with quartz-timer fuzes could be set to explode days after all terrorists had left the area. Gasoline pipelines transporting fuel to urban areas are also promising targets for terrorists. A pipeline would be relatively easy to repair, but destroying a pumping station would cause damage that would stop the flow until time-consuming repairs had been completed.

Gasoline storage tanks near urban areas are also vulnerable and poorly guarded. Security guards are prepared to stop drunken motorists from driving onto the premises, but would not be able to stop an armed terrorist team. Rupturing the tanks with explosives and setting the escaping fuel alight would produce fires that would be very difficult to extinguish. Depending on its equipment, the terrorists might not even have to force their way onto the premises. Rocket launchers make ideal weapons to use from outside a fence line against gasoline tanks, blasting open the tanks and setting fires simultaneously.

Another effect would be to choke off the area's gasoline supply. There would be rationing, and in areas without public transport the economic losses would be great because employees would not be able to report to work.

Liquefied natural gas, also known as "LNG," is even more dangerous than gasoline. LNG tankers have to unload far off-shore, because an accident could produce an explosion comparable to a small nuclear bomb.[22]

Public Places

Any place or event with large crowds is a potentially rewarding target for a terrorist. Confined places, such as air terminals, department stores, supermarkets, motion picture theaters, bars, restaurants, etc., are perfect for gas attacks or fire-bombs. Open areas, such as sports stadiums, parks and city streets are less ideal, but allow the use of gunfire coupled with a good chance of escape. Chemical weapons, such as nerve gas, are less effective in open areas. However, a terrorist who can employ a fuel-air weapon or a biological agent against a sports stadium can cause mass casualties.

Logging

Eco-terrorists have almost a free run of America's many forests, and make life difficult for loggers by driving 60-penny nails and plastic spikes into trees to damage the blades in sawmills. Despite increases in law enforcement and in private security in forests due for logging, the areas involved are so vast that tree spikers can work almost unmolested.

Construction Sabotage

Ecologists who object to new housing developments sometimes take dramatic steps to sabotage them. Others use low-key methods. Pulling up survey stakes brings the project to a halt and forces surveyors to repeat their work. A more subtle method is relocating stakes slightly, which if undetected can cause very expensive problems, because builders will have to demolish foundations and walls located in the wrong places.

Survey stakes used in road construction are especially vulnerable, because it's impractical to guard every foot of a projected roadway. Building construction sites often have night watchmen, which adds to the difficulty of sabotage.

Eco-terrorists have ways to sabotage heavy equipment, as well. Jamming ignition locks with toothpicks dipped in super glue, adding sand to motor oil, slashing tires, smashing fuel pumps and carburetors, and pouring a box of instant rice into the radiator are ways of disabling heavy equipment and forcing costly repairs.[23]

Monkeywrenching also includes miscellaneous harassment tactics. Eco-terrorists hate dirt bikers, and one tactic they suggest is to fill in dirt biker magazine subscription cards with the name and address of a furrier or local land developer.

The telephone is an avenue of attack. Printing fliers offering freebies and listing the telephone of a targeted business will tie up the lines with incoming calls. One terrorist-prankster used his computer to dial Jerry Falwell's

800-number repeatedly, running up a total of a half-million calls.[24]

Tearing down or burning advertising billboards is another type of vandalism eco-terrorists suggest. Because billboards are almost everywhere, they're very vulnerable to a variety of attacks.[25]

Stink bombs, using butyric acid or hydrogen sulfide, are for making business premises inhabitable. A stink bomb inside a retail outlet such as a fur store will force its closure until the odor clears.

Spray-painting a building, or the owners' residence or automobile is another harassment tactic. Other types of vandalism include jamming locks with super glue, and spilling raw sewage on carpeting.

Product Contamination

After seven people in Illinois died from cyanide-laced Extra-Strength Tylenol in 1982, product contamination became a widely recognized problem, although it had been taking place for many years. Before, and especially since, the Tylenol case, baby food jars turned up contaminated with broken glass. There have been instances of other types of contamination as well.

The Food and Drug Administration quarantined Chilean grapes after finding trace amounts of cyanide in two grapes. These had arrived in a shipment from the cargo ship Almeria Star, docked at Philadelphia. An unknown person, telephoning the American embassy in Santiago, had warned of the contamination. Federal inspectors found three Chilean grapes with puncture marks in Philadelphia, and two tested positive for cyanide. This led to the immediate recall of all Chilean fruit.[26]

In 1991, two people died, and one became seriously ill, after ingesting 12-Hour Sudafed capsules in Washington state, leading to a nationwide recall of the product. Physical evidence suggested that this was a case of supermarket tampering, not an "inside" job.[27] Eventually, a man was convicted of poisoning his wife, but the other poisoner(s) are still at large.

Britain seems to have been harder hit than the United States. Mars Bars, Pedigree Pet Foods, Hence, and Safeway are only four of the British firms victimized between 1984 and 1988 by extortionists who had threatened to, or actually contaminated food. In 1990, a jar of Heinz baby food was found with caustic soda and a pin contaminating its contents.[28]

Contaminating products on supermarket shelves is only one possibility. An "inside job," with a terrorist working for a food processing plant, can produce far-reaching results. Years ago, a harmless prank demonstrated the dangers. In the early 1980s, an employee put pornographic leaflets into Crackerjack boxes at the plant. These were distributed all over the country, and if they had been laced with a toxin, many people would have been poisoned before any countermeasures could have taken effect. Because of the time it takes for products to flow through the distribution network, the terrorist would have been long gone by the time the first casualties appeared.[29]

Miscellaneous Targets

Terrorists attack odd targets at times, depending on their purpose and ideology. One class of targets often attacked in recent years is businesses and laboratories using animals for research or animal products. Furriers, for example, have suffered damage, including arson and dyes poured on fur garments. University and private laboratories have been raided and damaged. One major attraction for terrorists is that security is so poor at these facilities. Furriers are on the alert for shoplifting and robbery, not sabotage. Laboratories usually do not have security directors. Overall, animal-rights targets are wide open and vulnerable.

During 1989, there were four attacks in the United States on bookstores carrying Salman Rushdie's *The Satanic Verses*. These were the only 1989 incidents on U.S. soil that met the State Department's definition of "international terrorist attacks."[30]

Terrorist attacks in response to Rushdie's book provide an excellent example of the far-reaching effects of terrorism, and how terrorists take advantage of the domino effect. While Rushdie was in hiding, guarded by British police, bookstore managers were agonizing over whether to withdraw his book. For almost a week, major booksellers such as Barnes & Noble and Waldenbooks did not display *The Satanic Verses* on their shelves. Only after protests by writers' organizations did they reverse their decision.[31] A few terrorist acts had produced a climate of fear.

The Climate of Fear

Soon after the Oklahoma City bombing of the federal building, there was a reappraisal of the vulnerabilities of federal buildings and courthouses around the country. This glass-fronted federal courthouse in Phoenix is obviously very vulnerable. (Photo by Tony Lesce.)

A destructive act, the threat of a destructive act, or even a bluff when conditions are right creates an atmosphere of anxiety and even panic. After a successful bombing, a telephoned bomb threat becomes more credible because it's impossible to dismiss or ignore. The targets are understandably very apprehensive if they survive, because of the prospect of another attack. After unknown persons fire-bombed the house of an African-American family in Berwyn, Illinois, both the family and neighbors became very apprehensive. A police car stood guard outside their house, and neighbors were concerned that it might happen again.[32]

An attack against one abortion clinic will result in enhanced security at many. Kidnapping an executive will cause many others to become apprehensive for their safety. This is the "ripple" or "domino" effect that multiplies the effectiveness of terrorists.[33]

Laying concrete barriers along the curb line in front of the Phoenix Federal Building assures that nobody can casually drive a truck through the front door. This is merely feel-good security, to reassure federal employees working in the building, as a truck bomb would devastate this glass-fronted building. (Photo by Tony Lesce.)

One immediate after-effect of the bombing of Sharon Rogers' Toyota van was that the headmaster at La Jolla County Day School told her that she could not return to her teaching job there. The school had received a bomb threat the day after the explosion, although no bomb had been found.[34] Other results were that Captain Rogers and his wife received protection from Naval Investigative Service bodyguards, and went into hiding.

Water treatment plants provide an example of fear overruling reason, and we see history repeating itself again and again. In 1968, radicals threatened to contaminate Chicago's water supply. This was pure bluff, but Chicago officials were in a near-panic. In 1972, there was a threat to contaminate one of New York City's water reservoirs, and the city's administrators panicked.[35] Officials believed that only a small amount of nerve gas would be sufficient, but later an army expert informed them that it would take tons of nerve gas to contaminate the reservoirs, which relieved the fear. Actually, contaminating a reservoir containing tens of millions of gallons of water requires a huge amount of poison, because a small amount would be so diluted that it would be harmless. Biological agents are very vulnerable to aeration and chlorination, standard water purification methods.

Another such incident took place in North Carolina in the 1970s, but no casualties resulted. The report on this incident is sketchy, not specifying the chemicals or their amounts, which makes it impossible to judge the seriousness of the problem.[36]

The Gulf War produced a rash of fears about water supply contamination. Los Angeles authorities closed a bike and jogging path around one reservoir in early 1991, and began closer scrutiny of employee I.D. around water plants. Washington, DC, officials stepped up the frequency of water testing. However, an expert pointed out the impracticality of poisoning the nation's water supplies.[37]

Despite the fears of officials, it's more practical to disrupt water delivery. When an aqueduct was dynamited in California in the 1970s, the destruction disrupted the Los Angeles water supply.[38]

World events can produce a climate of fear, even in the absence of any overt act. When the Gulf War was developing, there was widespread concern that terrorists would strike American shores. Security was enhanced at 435 U. S. airports and aboard 115 air carriers, according to the Federal Aviation Administration. Security officers at public places, including stadiums, airports and government buildings, scrutinized their beats for abandoned packages that might contain bombs.[39]

The tense Middle Eastern situation had a practical effect on some Americans planning to vacation in that region. Cancellation rates for tours varied from 10 percent to 50 percent.[40]

Airports, because of their extreme vulnerabilities, received a lot of attention. Some additional security measures included elimination of curbside check-in of luggage, and quick towing of unattended vehicles.[41]

A 1991 USA Today poll showed that 68 percent of Americans feared terrorist attacks. One expert warned that any place with crowds, such as office buildings, hotels, airports and train stations, were potential targets. One woman stated she was avoiding airports. Another even planned to evacuate her family from their Annendale, Virginia, home and head west.[42]

USA Today also interviewed citizens at different locales, eliciting their comments regarding their vulnerabilities. A Washington, DC, resident pointed to the Capitol, White House, and Federal Reserve as likely targets. South of Houston, Texas, a resident stated that the refineries would be "high risk" targets. The New York Stock Exchange, because of its vulnerability, was on alert, with more security guards augmenting the normal regime of I.D. badges, metal detectors, searches and multiple check-points. [43]

Fear produced some irrational responses. Officials delayed Continental Airlines Flight 16 in Honolulu because someone had found six batteries on a seat. Seeking the seat's occupant, officials stated that batteries "can be used to build a bomb on a plane."[44]

Predictably, some politicians took advantage of the situation to utter banal statements and vague threats. Senator William Cohen of Maine said that "Baghdad is now the terror capital of the world," and that Saddam Hussein would be "held accountable" for terrorist acts.[45]

Utah's Senator Orrin Hatch jumped on the bandwagon, predicting "a lot of terrorist acts." It was also a good time for "experts" to pontificate. Yonah Alexander was quoted as saying that Saddam's regime would live on in others' hearts and minds even after its destruction. Darrel Stephens of the Police Executive Research Forum also predicted terrorism.[46]

There were calmer opinions contemplating the terrorist campaign that never happened. Several terrorism experts cited in an article stated that they were not surprised that no wave of terrorism had hit America. Each laid out his own opinion regarding why terrorists had not, or had not yet, struck in the continental United States, but they were all right in one respect. The attacks never materialized.[47]

Police and potential victims tend to take threats very seriously. When there were death threats against Patrick Kennedy, campaigning in Rhode Island in 1994, authorities remembered what had happened to other members of his family. Three state troopers were assigned to guard the son of Senator Edward Kennedy as he campaigned for the post.[48]

Remembering the World Trade Center bombing also produced a reaction. A few days before the second anniversary of the bombing, police stepped up security on Wall Street. Officers stopped newspaper delivery trucks before letting them approach the New York Stock Exchange. Barricades prevented parking in front of the building, and visitors found their bags and parcels scrutinized. Police ordered an Italian food stand vendor to move his food stand away from the building. One employee stated outright that "People are scared."[49]

The Role of the Media

The media inadvertently collaborate with terrorists by providing publicity for their actions. The April 19, 1995, bombing of the federal office building in Oklahoma City was a media windfall. The TV channels were falling over each other trying to rivet viewers' attention, running bits of trivia interspersed with barrages of commercials. The hard news was very thin during the first few days. Most of the initial material on CNN was interviews with survivors, presenting accounts of how they were under a desk when they heard the boom and the roof caved in. One announcer promised much more news, so "stay with us." CNN even ran a view of the scene with the words "LIVE-EARLIER" at the top left of the screen.

Terrorists attain their ends with the active complicity of the media, as media outlets love to run sensational and tragic news. That's what grabs attention, and the media's job is to capture audiences for their advertisers.

In their efforts to deliver audiences to their advertisers, American mass media latch on to the most sensational subjects and bleed them to death, or at least until the ratings begin to drop. The competition for ratings ensures that any sensational act, from voyeurism to mass murder, will receive maximum publicity.

There is a well-rehearsed system for milking newsworthy events for maximum exposure. First, on-the-scene reporters are a must, even though they may not be able to provide any better coverage than a news reader sitting in front of a studio camera. Placing a reporter in front of the White House, for example, gives the illusion that the reporter has special access to the source of the news, even though the reporter may be reading from the same press release handed out to every media representative by the White House Press Office.

Another tactic is the interview, whether it's anyone worth interviewing or not. In some cases, news at first is sparse, which is when reporters will begin interviewing each other at the scene and speculating on imminent developments. We saw some of this during the first few days of coverage of the Oklahoma City bombing, when hard news was very thin.

Not far behind is the interview with an expert. This may be a real expert, such as the chief investigator on the case, or it may be a synthetic "expert," such as a psychologist or psychiatrist who has lectured on serial killers, skyjackers or terrorists. Some may be members of "think tanks" or "research institutes." Interviewers gloss over the fact that most of these "experts" have never met a serial killer or bomber.

One "terrorism expert" expressed the opinion that "I think there's been an informal bond between terrorists and their victims not to exceed certain constraints — chemical, radiological, nuclear and biological weapons. Now the terrorists have begun to exceed this contract."[50] How this expert was able to determine the nature of the "bond" or "contract" was not explained. The article also did not state how many terrorists or victims he had interviewed to draw this conclusion.

Public opinion polls are also part of the news picture. True to form, the media early on conducted "polls" to measure Americans' beliefs about the Oklahoma City bombing. It's amazing how they try to measure the unknowable, such as whether the bombers will get caught, quizzing people who are totally uninvolved and unconnected with the event or investigation. One Gallup poll asked precisely that. It also asked if it appears that there will be more bombings, and almost half the people polled said "no." It is frightening that we choose our presidents this way as well.

Strident media attention ensures that there will be more bombings, and, as usual, the perpetrators will be hard to find, for the obvious reason that the evidence self-destructs. It may get to the point where a bombing is merely routine. A TV station might begin the morning news with "And here's the list of yesterday's bombings... after these messages."

"Copy-cat" crimes occur when the media sensationalize and over-report a crime. This is the phenomenon police officers fear, because the high-tension reporting inspires the community's weak-minded crazies to get their share of the attention by imitating the original bomber, rapist or shooter. As we'll see in the chapter on bombings, New York City suffered an epidemic of bombings during the late 1950s when the media played up the "Mad Bomber."

A more recent copy-cat occurrence was a result of the sensationalized reporting of the gunman who killed and injured several people in abortion clinics in late December, 1994. An Oregon man equipped himself with a shotgun and two pipe bombs in January, 1995. He set fire to a store and tried to get a bus driver to take him to an abortion clinic. An indicator of the man's mental state is that there are no abortion clinics in the area. The man then invaded a school district office, and was disarmed in a struggle with a wrestling coach. The shotgun wounded the man during the struggle.[51]

The Hidden Costs of Terrorism

Sabotage and destruction result in extra costs, not only to repair the damage, but to implement extra security. Security costs come both in money and time, such as the extra delay imposed on airline passengers by airport security measures. The net result is that anti-terrorism measures increase the already existing friction in our society.

Animal-rights activists broke into University of Arizona laboratories in 1989 to free test animals and destroy equipment. They caused $250,000 in damage, but the university spent $800,000 for additional security.

Militant animal-rights activism began in Britain, where campaigns have been more far-reaching than their American counterparts. In one campaign, activists stated that they had poisoned Mars candy bars, because Mars was involved with animal experiments. This caused the company financial loss because of product recalls, even though it was a hoax.

One result of anti-abortion terrorism has been increased security at abortion clinics. Planned Parenthood, with 900 centers and a staff of 22,000, spends tens of millions of dollars for security, 20 percent of its $500 million yearly budget. Admitting that this security alone won't solve the problem, Planned Parenthood's president Pamela Maraldo asked for more federal help.[52]

The aircraft skyjackings of the 1960s resulted in the installation of permanent security checkpoints at all major airports and most minor ones. This required purchasing barriers, X-ray conveyer belts, and metal detectors. It also involved hiring security personnel to operate the new equipment, and assigning police officers on a permanent basis to back up security officers. The annual cost of airport security in the United States is several billion dollars.

New measures against airborne bombs cost millions of dollars yearly, and delay passengers even more than before. This is part of the increased friction that is the fallout of terrorism.

Some nations are truly besieged by terrorism, and terrorism countermeasures dominate daily life. Britain has suffered terrorism as a result of the war in Northern Ireland, and there are checkpoints in major department stores, public places and airports. Israeli life is shaped around personal and national security. In both countries, there is great fear of bombs.

The Israeli Example:
It Could Happen Here

Israel has many terrorists already within its borders, and more enter daily. Israeli embassies, consulates and other facilities around the world have been assaulted by Middle Eastern attackers. Space allows listing only a few highlights:

In June, 1982, there was an attempt on the life of Shlomo Argov, Israeli Ambassador to Great Britain in London. The ambassador survived, but the attack was yet another reason for strict security precautions at all Israeli diplomatic posts.

There may have been an element of tit-for-tat in this attack, because Jewish Defense League extremists took credit for a bomb attached to a Soviet diplomat's car in New York City in September, 1981. As sponsors of Arab terrorism, the Soviets may have quietly passed the word.

Rabbi Meir Kahane, founder of New York's Jewish Defense League, was shot to death in a New York hotel in 1990. Kahane's shooting was obviously one more step in the game of mutual reprisals both sides have been playing for years. Whatever the case, Kahane supporters vowed "revenge."

Sol Margolis, president of Kach International, the extremist group founded by Kahane, stated "There will be revenge. We believe in revenge," according to *USA Today*. The following day, two elderly Palestinians were murdered in Israel's occupied territories, and police suspected it was "retaliatory."[53]

The Israelis continued to be targets, both inside and outside their country. A car bomb exploded outside the Israeli embassy in Buenos Aires, Argentina, in March, 1992, killing 20 and injuring 240 others. A Lebanese group claimed credit for the explosion.[54]

The immediate effects of this were many, extending to neighboring Brazil. Police blocked the street in front of a Sao Paulo synagogue, searched members of the congregation with metal detectors, and conducted physical searches as well. Other Jewish organizations received special police protection.

In Israel today, the atmosphere is paranoid. Any un-attended suitcase, package, shopping bag or other object in a bus station, airport, market or other public place provokes a call to the police, because Israelis are deathly afraid of bombs, following a series of bus bombs in 1994 and 1995.

At this point, the United States is not quivering in fear of terrorist attacks. A wave of such attacks could make security the dominant issue, and people may become frightened enough to tolerate and even insist upon security measures that would interfere with daily life.

America's Diminishing Immunity

The reason foreign terrorists haven't been more active in the United States is simply distance. Arab terrorists, for example, don't have to travel thousands of miles when the main irritant and target, American-backed Israel, is right next door. American air carriers fly literally all over the world. American embassies are in almost every duchy and sheikdom and within convenient reach. As we've seen, this is changing, because Middle Eastern terrorism is spilling over onto American soil. We contribute to this through our foreign policy.

Anti-American Sentiment

Over the years, we've seen a plethora of news reports about demonstrations in front of American embassies and overseas offices of American corporations. Demonstrators have protested social conditions, nuclear armaments, racial strife in the United States, and other issues. Of course, this brings up the difficult question: "Why do so many foreigners hate us?" More to the point, why do they hate us despite the billions in foreign aid we've laid out for them?

The background to this situation is clear. The United States government has been playing "Big Brother" to many of the world's smaller nations. As for foreign aid, this usually takes the form of direct aid to despots ruling foreign countries, and it doesn't trickle down to the large mass of citizens of these countries. Giving a South American or Asian dictator guns and tanks to fight against his own people isn't the sort of foreign aid that makes friends among citizens of those countries.

An extraordinarily good example that works differently is aid to Israel. Economic and military aid to a country at odds with all of its neighbors can't help but produce profound resentment among the neighbors. These are the same Arabs upon whom we depend for cheap petroleum, and whose oil we consume to avoid depleting our strategic stockpiles.

It seems illogical to provide aid to Israel, knowing that this will antagonize Israel's neighbors, upon whom we depend for oil, but the powerful American Jewish lobby has an influence far exceeding its small number of members. Any legislator opposing aid to Israel risks being labeled "anti-semitic," with the Jewish lobby contributing to his opponent in the next election. This is the practical result of a group of Americans who appear to owe their primary allegiance to a foreign power.

The Middle East provides an excellent example of a totally irrational American foreign policy which, instead of making friends, only produces enemies by antagonizing everyone. The United States' support of the Shah of Iran antagonized religious fundamentalists and other Iranians who realized the corrupt nature of the Shah's regime. Once the revolutionaries deposed the Shah, they vented their dislike of the United States by capturing the American Embassy and holding its personnel hostage in 1979 and 1980. This determined American policy during the Iraq-Iran War.

The United States gave aid to Saddam Hussein's Iraq, on the logic that "The enemy of my enemy is my friend." This confirmed Iran's enmity, but when the Iraqi invasion of Kuwait took place, the United States sided against Saddam Hussein and led the Gulf War coalition. Possibly this was partly because an Iraqi fighter lobbed two missiles into the destroyer U.S.S. Stark by mistake one night during the Iran-Iraq War, but if this incident had an influence, it was unfortunate. During the 1967 Israeli conflict, Israeli jets and motor gunboats attacked the U.S.S. Liberty in broad daylight in international waters. The Israelis claimed that the attack, which lasted several hours and produced many American casualties, was a "mistake," and the United States did not retaliate.

In 1985, when the American citizen Jonathan Pollard was convicted of spying for Israel against his own country, the United States did not impose any sanctions against Israel. The lesson was clear to Arab nations, however. The United States has a special relationship with Israel, and excuses warlike acts by Israel against the United States.

Between inept American politicians and the American Jewish lobby, our Middle Eastern policy has lurched from being friendly to one faction to trying to be friends with all. In the Byzantine and treacherous Middle Eastern political environment, there's no hope of that. Instead, we've made enemies of them all.

Given this background, it's not surprising that Middle Eastern Arabs assassinate and kidnap American government and corporate officials, bomb American embassies, and generally despise us. In one sense, our foreign outposts serve another purpose, that of providing accessible targets for hate. They are lightning rods that attract the destruction that otherwise would find its way to our shores. In recent years, we've seen this pattern begin to shift.

Security

Protection against terrorism is almost impossible. The plain fact is that "security" is point defense, and our systems are vulnerable at too many points to protect.

Even point defense is flawed and imperfect, because even the tightest security screen is porous. For an example, let's examine the security around the White House in the next chapter.

Notes:

1. "Japan-Subway: History of Terrorist Attacks," Associated Press, March 20, 1995.
2. *Disruptive Terrorism*, Santoro, Victor, Port Townsend, WA, Loompanics Unlimited, 1984, p. 28.
3. *Ibid.*, p. 38.
4. *Technological Terrorism*, Clark, Richard C., Old Greenwich, CT, Devin-Adair Company, 1980, p. 126.
5. *Disruptive Terrorism*, Santoro, Victor, Port Townsend, WA, Loompanics Unlimited, 1984, p. 41.
6. Waltman, James V., "Voice Mail Security: Get The Message," *Security Management*, Volume 39, No. 5, May, 1995, p. 36.
7. Howlett, Debbie, "USA's Transit 'Time Bombs;' Chicago Flooding Was Tip of Iceberg," *USA Today*, April 29, 1992, p. 1A.
8. Schmid, Randolph E., "Transit Threat: Mass Transit Vulnerable to Terrorism," Associated Press, March 22, 1995.
9. Meddis, Sam Vincent, and Curley, Tom, "'Gestapo' Tactic: Train Attack," *USA Today*, October 10, 1995, p. 3A.
10. *Disruptive Terrorism*, Santoro, Victor, Port Townsend, WA, Loompanics Unlimited, 1984, p. 63.

11. *Ecodefense: A Field Guide to Monkeywrenching*, Second Edition, Foreman, Dave, and Haywood, Bill, Tucson, AZ, Ned Ludd Books, 1987, pp. 92-96.
12. "Off-road Race Course Sabotaged," Associated Press, May 29, 1991.
13. *Ecodefense: A Field Guide to Monkeywrenching*, Second Edition, Foreman, Dave, and Haywood, Bill, Tucson, AZ, Ned Ludd Books, 1987, pp. 100-103.
14. *Terrorism*, Holms, John Pynchon, and Burke, Tom, New York, Pinnacle Books, 1994, pp. 205-206.
15. *Ibid.*, pp. 50-51.
16. Magnuson, Ed, "Ten Minutes of Horror," *Time*, January 6, 1986.
17. Kovsky, Steve, "Corporate Terrorism, A New Global Threat," *Management Review*, v79, n10, October, 1990, p. 39.
18. *Ecodefense: A Field Guide to Monkeywrenching*, Second Edition, Foreman, Dave, and Haywood, Bill, Tucson, AZ, Ned Ludd Books, 1987, pp. 74-75.
19. McConnell, Beth, "Study Urges Utilities to Boost Deterrence Against Terrorist or Weather Threats," *The Energy Report*, v18, n 27, July 16, 1990, p. 399.
20. Information received from a security specialist who is an acquaintance of the author's, and works in a related security field.
21. *The Silent Brotherhood*, Flynn, Kevin, and Gerhardt, Gary, New York, The Free Press, 1989, p. 389.
22. *Technological Terrorism*, Clark, Richard C., Old Greenwich, CT, Devin-Adair Company, 1980, p. 126.
23. *Ecodefense: A Field Guide to Monkeywrenching*, Second Edition, Foreman, Dave, and Haywood, Bill, Tucson, AZ, Ned Ludd Books, 1987, pp. 117-140.
24. *Ibid.*, p 220.
25. *Ibid.*, pp. 221-234.
26. Carlson, Margaret, "Do You Dare To Eat A Peach?" *Time*, March 27, 1989, p. 24.

27. "Sudafed Capsules Recalled in Wake of 2 Cyanide Deaths," Associated Press, March 4, 1991.
28. Withington, John, "Terrorism on the High Street," *Management Today*, January, 1990, p. 56.
29. *Disruptive Terrorism*, Santoro, Victor, Port Townsend, WA, Loompanics Unlimited, 1984, p. 88.
30. Kovsky, Steve, "Corporate Terrorism, A New Global Threat," *Management Review*, v79, n10, October, 1990, p. 39.
31. Smith, William E., "The New Satans," *Time*, March 6, 1989, p. 36.
32. Johnson, Kevin, "Family's 'Real Life' Racism; Whites are Divided Over Black Neighbors," *USA Today*, March 13, 1992, p. 3A.
33. *Disruptive Terrorism*, Santoro, Victor, Port Townsend, WA, Loompanics Unlimited, 1984, p. 124.
34. "The Exile of Sharon Rogers," *Time*, April 7, 1989, p. 27.
35. *The New York Daily News*, February 14, 1977.
36. *Technological Terrorism*, Clark, Richard C., Old Greenwich, CT, Devin-Adair Company, 1980, p. 113.
37. Kanamine, Linda, "Water Officials Fear Plants Are Vulnerable," *USA Today*, January 24, 1991, p. 6A.
38. *Technological Terrorism*, Clark, Richard C., Old Greenwich, CT, Devin-Adair Company, 1980, p. 124.
39. Squitieri, Tom, "Security: The Word of the Hour," *USA Today*, January 19, 1991, p. 9A.
40. Trippett, Frank, "They'd Rather be In Philadelphia," *Time*, September 17, 1990, p. 69.
41. Meddis, Sam, "USA Combats 'Real Threat' of Terrorism," *USA Today*, January 18, 1991, p. 1A.
42. Peterson, Karen S., "Question Gnaws: Will Terrorists Hit Here?" *USA Today*, January 19, 1991, p. 4D.
43. Stone, Andrea, "Fear of Terrorism Runs Wide, Deep," *USA Today*, January 19, 1991, p. 9A.
44. Squitieri, Tom, "Security: The Word of the Hour," *USA Today*, January 19, 1991, p. 9A.

45. Meddis, Sam, "FBI Very Alert For Terrorism," *USA Today*, September 27, 1990, p. 4A.
46. Meddis, Sam, "Terrorism Threat Real, Lasting; Expect to See Tighter Security," *USA Today*, January 18, 1991, p. 9A.
47. Cauchon, Dennis, "Strategy; Lack of Terrorism Not Surprising," *USA Today*, February 11, 1991, p. 4A.
48. "Kennedy Death Threats Worry State Police," Associated Press, November 9, 1994.
49. Hays, Tom, "Trade Center Bombing: Wall Street Security Heightened," Associated Press, February 14, 1995.
50. Hampson, Rick, "Progress Offers Up Tools of Terrorism," Associated Press, March 21, 1995.
51. Barnard, Jeff, "School Gunman Burns Store, Threatens School, Gets Shot," Associated Press, January 19, 1995.
52. "Clinic Shooting: Planned Parenthood Says Tightened Security Alone Won't Stop Violence," Associated Press, December 31, 1994.
53. Greene, Marilyn, "Supporters Vow Revenge for Kahane," *USA Today*, November 7, 1990, p. 1A.
54. Katz, Lee Michael, "Lebanese Group Says It Set Bomb," *USA Today*, March 19, 1992, p. 4A.

Chapter Five
Case Study:
The White House

The President of the United States is one of the most well-guarded men in the world. He and his family don't have to worry about getting mugged, or having a homeless person accost them and slobber over their clothing while begging for a handout. Yet, both presidential security and the White House security system have gaps.

There have been recent news accounts of attacks against the White House. The first was the man who crashed a light plane on the South Lawn one night during September, 1994. Another was the man who fired shots from a rifle at the White House one afternoon in November, 1994. In December, several shots, including one 9mm bullet that penetrated a State Dining Room window, struck the White House in what might well have been a "drive-by" shooting. A homeless man wielding a knife was shot down by a Park Police officer outside the White House fence.[1]

A few days later, on December 23, a man carrying an automatic pistol was arrested after officers saw him "skulking" on the Ellipse near the White House. Barely an hour later, officers arrested a man who had pulled his car over by the White House fence. After being accosted by Park Police and Secret Service officers, the man said his car contained a plutonium bomb. A search showed that the car did not contain any explosives. That these incidents followed each other so closely must be causing the Secret Service bodyguards great concern. One reason is copycat crimes.[2]

This concern is justified, because in May, 1995, another man scaled the fence around the White House and approached it with a revolver in his hand. Secret Service agents and White House officers confronted the man, and one officer fired during the scuffle, hitting both the intruder and another officer.[3]

A copy-cat jumped the White House fence only three days after the first. This man, with no fixed address, was unarmed, but was arrested and charged.

President Clinton isn't very popular. Probably, fewer people like him today than when he was elected, with only 43 percent of those who voted choosing him. It takes only one person, with a gun, knife, or light plane, to carry out an attack on the White House or the president when he's away from home. One who succeeded was Lee Harvey Oswald, whom the Secret Service will never forget, because they're very aware that it could happen again.

It doesn't help at all to dismiss these attackers as deranged individuals. If the bullet finds its target, labeling the shooter as "disorganized" or "mentally ill" becomes irrelevant to the victim. To the Secret Service, it's no doubt frightening how close some of these people came to success, despite their alleged mental problems.

It is also noteworthy that the media, after the initial news reports of the attacks on the White House, fell silent on both topics: attacks and presidential security. There was no long series of "analyses" by media pundits regarding the adequacy of presidential security. Perhaps the Secret Service, someone else in the government, or even a conclave of top media people who determine editorial policy, decided that this would be a restricted topic. The reason? Simple: The phenomenon of "copycat crimes" is well-known. When the media publicize a sensational and bizarre criminal, they inspire other weak-minded and suggestible people to do the same. The Secret Service doesn't need other people with access to a firearm or a light plane attacking the White House.

However, the media feel free to play up other bizarre crimes to the hilt; after all, it's only the little people who get hurt by the likes of Jeffrey Dahmer and John Wayne Gacy. Media owners really don't care about that. In fact, it boosts audiences when they have more sensational crimes to play up in the usual lurid manner.

Protection: Fact and Fiction

The Secret Service, understandably, is normally tight-lipped regarding their protective measures. This allows imaginative journalists free rein to write some pretty out-landish things, since they won't be contradicted by any authoritative source.

This serves the purpose of the Secret Service. If potential attackers believe that the defensive measures are total and impenetrable, this may deter attacks. Over the years, there have been in print statements that the Secret Service examines every window (false) on the route of a presidential motorcade, and orders them all shut while the president is passing. One imaginative account years ago stated that the Secret Service warned occupants of offices overlooking the route that they would open fire at any window they saw open. This obviously isn't so, because people were hanging out of windows along President Kennedy's Dallas motorcade route. Lee Harvey Oswald had easy access to one of these windows when he fired at President Kennedy.

Another story that's been appearing occasionally for years is that the Secret Service placed agents with Stinger missiles on the roof of the White House, with orders to shoot at any aircraft that gets within a certain range. This, too, is obviously false, as it would generate a scandal if an agent fired a missile in error and it crashed through the window of a nearby building or came down in the street. Likewise, if an airliner were shot down while straying near the White House, it could crash into crowded Washington, DC, streets with great loss of life. In any case, no Stinger missiles were fired at the aircraft that crashed onto the White House lawn. In fact, agents did not become aware that the aircraft was heading their way until the last few seconds.

Closing Pennsylvania Avenue in front of the White House to motor traffic was a step in the right direction, although it will have only a slight effect. The president remains vulnerable, because the White House is not truly a fortress, and he has to leave it for many public appearances. All successful attacks on the president took place outside the White House.

The bottom line is that historically every successful presidential attacker was a lone gunman with limited resources. The only attempt involving more than one person was Collazzo and Torresola's attack upon Blair House in 1950, and it failed totally.

That was then; this is now. News photographs of various presidents, taken through the windows of the Oval Office, show that he is at times visible from outside. Even with bullet-resistant glass in all of the White House windows, they're very vulnerable to attacks from rocket launchers. This isn't the only likely form of attack.

The Secret Service and the president apparently take these threats very seriously. Recently enacted security enhancements, such as closing off Pennsylvania Avenue in front of the White House, show that they have grave concerns. Recent events justify these precautions. Steps have been taken to guard against a variety of projected attacks, including sorties by remote-controlled ultralight aircraft carrying explosives or toxins, or balloons with destructive payloads.

We've seen teams of Middle Eastern and home-grown terrorists mount successful and very lethal attacks, the bombings of the World Trade Center and the Oklahoma City Alfred P. Murrah Federal Building being two examples. Terrorists carried out a 1991 mortar attack on Britain's Number Ten Downing Street. It's not too hard to imagine that a well-coordinated attack on the White House, involving suicide bombers and commandos, would have a very good chance of success. It's an ominous portent that a recent novel, *Warriors of God*, outlined exactly this sort of attack. Considering the way terrorist attacks have imitated art, this describes a serious threat, and the president's Secret Service guards would be remiss if they did not consider such a possibility.

Suicide and other types of bombers are the topic of the next chapter. Bombing attacks are becoming more frightening, although still relatively rare.

Notes:

1. Fournier, Ron, "White House Shooting: More Gunfire at White House: Police Shoot Man With Knife," Associated Press, December 20, 1994.
2. Benac, Nancy, "White House Arrests: Arrests Multiply in Unrelated Incidents," Associated Press, December 23, 1994.
3. Fournier, Ron, "Gunman Wounded at White House," Associated Press, May 24, 1995.

Chapter Six
Bombings

Bombs are weapons of stealth, because they're easy to set and forget. They're impersonal, because the bomber can walk away before the detonation takes place, or can mail them to remote locations. They destroy themselves, and the evidence goes up with them.[1]

Police officers are looking a little more closely at parked rental trucks these days. (Photo by Tony Lesce.)

Bombs have long been favorite weapons among several foreign terrorist groups. The Irish Republican Army used a car bomb to kill British Member of Parliament Airey Neave in the Houses of Parliament garage. They killed Ian Gow, another

MP, with a bomb wired to his car in July, 1990. The IRA had also bombed the London Stock Exchange on July 20, 1990, and a few days later, killed three police officers and a nun in Ulster with a land mine.[2]

In the United States, bombs are weapons of both political terrorists and unstable individuals. Opponents of the civil-rights movement of the 1950s and 1960s sometimes used explosives to strike at their enemies. Frank Johnson, the federal judge who ruled that Alabama's segregated buses were illegal, found himself on the receiving end. A bomber partly destroyed his mother's house during a 1992 attempt on Johnson's life.[3]

New York City experienced an epidemic of bombings during the middle 1950s, when the publicity over George Metesky, the "Mad Bomber," led to a plethora of imitators. The media awarded each his own cute sobriquet, and New York suffered from the "Sunday Bomber," the "Weekend Bomber," the "Subway Bomber," the "Bathroom Bomber," the "Staten Island Ferry Bomber," the "42nd Street Bomber," and many others.

FALN, the Puerto Rican separatist movement, planted a bomb in New York City's Fraunces Tavern on January 24, 1975, killing four and injuring 50 people. By contrast, New York City's "Mad Bomber" was a disaffected former utility employee nursing a grudge that he'd been unfairly treated. It's significant that, despite the Mad Bomber's allegedly unstable mental condition, he was able to pursue a 16-year-long career, eluding the police until a massive investigation uncovered his name and samples of his handwriting in the utility company's files. This led to his apprehension and confinement in a mental hospital.

Bombing incidents have been increasing in the United States. In 1988, there were 1,108 explosive incidents, killing 60 people and injuring 691. In 1992, there were 2,493 incidents, which claimed somewhat fewer casualties, 45 killed and 469 injured.[4]

This building is appallingly vulnerable to a truck bomb because of the glass front and the curb line only feet in front of the glass. (Photo by Tony Lesce.)

The glass front in this building is farther away from the curb line, but still very vulnerable to a large bomb. (Photo by Tony Lesce.)

A compelling reason for the increase in bombings in this country is the availability of materials for building improvised explosive devices (IED). Supermarkets and hardware stores sell these materials openly, and the would-be bomber can obtain them with far less hassle and risk of detection than buying a firearm. It takes minimal skill to put together a homemade bomb.[5] George Metesky, New York's "Mad Bomber," improvised his pipe bombs using plumbing pipe and the propellant from shotgun shells.

Motives for bombings vary from political to personal. There have been well over 150 incidents of abortion clinic bombings. There have also been over 100 drug-related incidents. Other apparently politically motivated bombings involved homes, vehicles, businesses, schools and police stations.

This building is somewhat less vulnerable because of its small windows, even though the parking area and curb line are still uncomfortably close. (Photo by Tony Lesce.)

Animal-Rights Bombings

Animal-rights activists sometimes become bomb terrorists. One woman was arrested after placing a pipe bomb outside a surgical instruments company. The bomb did not explode, but arresting officers found three other pipe bombs in her apartment. [6]

Civil-Rights Bombings

The resurgence of attacks against civil-rights figures in more dangerous forms is evident. Judge Robert Vance was killed by a nail-studded mail bomb in December, 1989. The same month, an African-American civil-rights attorney in Savannah, Georgia, was the victim of a similar device. In January, 1991, another nail-filled bomb arrived in the mail of a minister of a mixed-race church. The explosion injured his daughter, who opened the package. Two similar bombs that failed to explode arrived at Atlanta, Georgia's 11th Circuit Court of Appeals and the Jacksonville, Florida, office of the National Association for the Advancement of Colored People, (NAACP). [7]

Other bombs exploded around the same time outside the door of the Bureau of Indian Affairs in Riverside, California, and at the Morongo Indian reservation nearby. These appeared to have no relation to the bombs in the Southeast states. A letter sent to an Atlanta TV station by a group calling itself "Americans for a Competent Federal Judicial System" threatened further bombings. The letter claimed that the judicial system is more lenient towards blacks who attack whites. [8]

Civil-rights issues are still with us. An African-American family, recently arrived in the white working-class Chicago suburb of Berwyn in 1992, found themselves harassed and fire-bombed in their new home. [9]

The *Cincinnati Herald*, written for the African-American community, received threatening phone calls after running an article on Arab Muslims in March, 1994. After several threats, an unidentified person threw a plastic bottle filled with gasoline into a newsroom window, where it caused about $12,000 worth of damage.[10]

Miscellaneous Bombings

For no discernible reason, someone set five bombs in Indiana at about the same time. The first bomb killed a man on December 23, 1990, but nobody was hurt in the other blasts. Most bombs were placed near gas meters at apartment buildings.[11]

Early the next month, six pipe bombs turned up on two fuel and methanol tanks near the Norfolk, Virginia, Naval Base. These were crude devices, suggesting that they were not the work of professional terrorists but amateurs.[12]

The FBI continued to investigate, but eventually ran into a dead end. Authorities were unable to link the bombs to terrorists, nor apparently to anyone else.[13] Unlike on the movie and TV screens, real-life investigations often dribble away into oblivion.

Types Of Bombs

Bombs come in all shapes and sizes, degrees of explosive power, and levels of sophistication. Crude bombs, easily built by a high-school drop-out with or without a rudimentary knowledge of chemistry, can be as deadly as elaborately fuzed special-purpose bombs.

There are several categories of explosives available, ranging from low explosives to high explosives, the difference being the burning rate. The differences are easy to understand without getting too technical.

"Black powder" uses combustion, and consists of a fuel and an oxidizer to support the burning, which produces gas, heat, flame, and a lot of smoke. If the gunpowder is confined, pressure builds up in the container and it eventually ruptures, producing the blast. Unconfined black powder merely burns with a hot flame.

High explosives such as TNT and RDX don't burn in the usual sense. The effect comes from the disintegration of the chemical molecules, and high explosives explode whether in the open or confined in a container. The speed at which the reaction takes place is much faster with high explosives, which makes them much more effective for demolition. A pound of black powder placed against a brick wall, for example, would merely burn, unless confined inside a vessel that caused the pressure to build up. On the other hand, a pound of high explosive would immediately detonate with such shattering force that it would punch a large hole through the wall.

This shattering force is called "brisance," and high explosives are rated for brisance. Some high explosives have more shattering power, or brisance, than others, and produce a sharper, more abrupt explosion.

"Plastic explosives" are high explosives, but are soft like clay or putty. This allows shaping the charge to fit in small spaces, and to fit around an object to be destroyed, such as a bridge girder. Plastic explosives are favorites with terrorists, and one type often used is "Semtex," made in Czechoslovakia. Semtex was the explosive in the bomb that blew Pan Am Flight 103 out of the air over Lockerbie. Libya bought 1,000 tons of Semtex during the 1980s, and some of it has seeped into terrorist pipelines.

High explosives can be improvised, one example being the ammonium nitrate and fuel oil mixture popular with bombers. These improvised explosives aren't as powerful as conventional high explosives, but they're adequate for the task.

Gunpowder, or smokeless powder, is the propellant used in cartridges, and is similar in composition to high explosives.

Gunpowder contains ingredients called "deterrents," such as carbon, to slow the reaction. This is necessary because otherwise the pressure would build up too quickly and shatter the gun barrel. Unconfined, gunpowder simply burns with a bright, hot flame, producing little smoke.

Confining gunpowder produces the same effect as confining black powder — an explosion when the rapidly increasing pressure ruptures the container. Bomb makers who use improvised explosives such as gunpowder use a container such as plumbing pipe to confine the gas until the pressure is high enough to break open the pipe and produce a blast.

There's another type of explosive that has received little mention or use until recently, although its effects have been known for a very long time. This is the fuel-air explosive, and is a combustible agent dispersed in air. Any fine powder, such as flour, will produce an explosion when floating in air. Flour mills have suffered explosions because there is often a fine haze of flour floating in the air, and a stray spark or flame can ignite it with devastating effects. Today, flour mills use forced ventilation and ground all electrical appliances to avoid this danger.

Gasoline is another fuel that can produce a devastating explosion when vaporized. In liquid form, gasoline isn't terribly dangerous, and it's possible to drop a lighted cigarette into a bucket of gasoline without even producing a flame. But gasoline vapor is extremely flammable, with an explosive effect. In the open, a burning cloud of gasoline produces an effect visually similar to a miniature nuclear explosion: a fireball, shock wave, and a mushroom-shaped cloud. Confined, as inside a structure, the shock wave has an explosive effect.

Availability

Manufactured bombs and explosive devices are available in armed forces arsenals, and there are enough militants in the armed forces to sneak a number of these out to their groups.

There are so many grenades, rockets and explosive devices in the armed forces' inventories that it's impossible to keep track of them all. At times, some of these illicit supplies come to the surface. In Connecticut in 1995, police stopped a camouflage-painted truck and found it was carrying hand grenades, mortars, and rocket propelled grenades, known as "RPGs."[14]

High explosives, such as dynamite, are available almost everywhere, but buyers usually have to show I. D. and sign for them. Military explosives, such as RDX, are usually made under contract for the armed forces, and are unavailable on the open civilian market.

Components for improvised explosives, such as gasoline, ammonium nitrate, and fuel oil, are commonly available. The frightening aspect of this picture is that the most versatile substance, gasoline, is available everywhere in the country and with practically no controls on its purchase. Further, no practical controls are possible, leaving the door wide open to terrorists wanting to make a fuel-air bomb or a fire-bomb.

Pipe Bombs

Pipe bombs are made of plumbing pipe, with end caps, and can be very simple. New York's Mad Bomber cut open shotgun shells to obtain the active ingredient for his pipe bombs, using a simple flame fuze to cause detonation after he'd left the scene.

Some makers of pipe bombs use them to detonate a larger explosive or combustible charge, or wrap scrap metal around them for enhanced fragmentation. Nails, bolts and nuts provide excellent fragments which can kill or cause serious injuries.

Bombs made of pipe and/or bottles comprised about 85 percent of the bombs used in 1992, probably because they're so easy to make.[15] One type of low-powered bomb used by teenage pranksters is the mailbox bomb, a plastic bottle which is filled with water and dry ice and placed in a curbside mailbox as a practical joke in bad taste.

Mail and Letter Bombs

Letter bombs are thick envelopes containing a couple of ounces of high explosive and a fuze. Mail bombs can be packages of various sizes, depending on their contents. All are designed to detonate when opened, and the more sophisticated bombs have anti-tamper switches, to frustrate an explosive ordnance officer trying to disarm them.

In theory, mail bombs are very selective, because they're addressed to specific persons. In practice, some mail bombs are opened by the target's relative, secretary, or a mail clerk. Some poorly made letter and package bombs detonate prematurely, injuring post office employees.

Lay-off and Culvert Bombs

Bombs planted by the roadside or in culverts under a road are useful for remote-control attacks and for delaying road traffic. The lay-off bomb is a heavy charge planted near or under a road. The site can be inside a man-hole, mailbox, or even a building. If the situation makes it practical, terrorists can dig a hole next to the road and bury the bomb. A wired or wireless fuze detonates the bomb when the target vehicle is next to it. Triggering the bomb requires an observer close enough to see the position, but far enough away to be safe from the blast.

The lay-off bomb is effective only when the terrorist knows the route and approximate timing. If the target regularly appears at the same point at about the same time because he commutes, terrorists can use a lay-off bomb to destroy him, his vehicle, and his bodyguards. A motorcade is an ideal target for a lay-off bomb. This is why presidential bodyguards often remove mailboxes and seal manholes before a motorcade.

Culvert bombs can also be fuzed by a remote control. A few of these can delay traffic, especially military convoys, because it becomes necessary to search every possible hiding place before allowing traffic to proceed.

Boobytraps

A boobytrap is a device triggered by the target's action, such as opening a door, flipping a light switch, or even flushing a toilet. Boobytraps come in all shapes and sizes, and are not necessarily high explosives. A booby-trap that drenches the target in gasoline, then ignites the fuel, is just as effective as a bomb.

One type of boobytrap sent through the mail was the rigged Walkman tape player used in South Africa in 1991. The bomber had addressed the package to Dirk Coetzee, a former police officer who had moved to Zambia, and showed extraordinary cleverness in listing a civil-rights lawyer as the return address. Coetzee refused the package because he'd have had to pay import duty, and the post office returned it to the "sender," Bheki Mlangheni, at his office. Mlangheni took it home with him and put on the headset. When he hit the "PLAY" button, the right earphone exploded.[16]

Human imagination is the only limit to the form a boobytrap can take. A box of candy, ignition switch, brake pedal, doorknob, desk drawer, or refrigerator door can be rigged to set off a destructive device. It's possible to rig almost any object to trigger a boobytrap, although it's not possible to guarantee that the target will trigger it. Boobytraps are indiscriminate, and someone else may perform the act that triggers a particular device. Despite this shortcoming, some terrorists still employ boobytraps.

Truck Bombs

For this discussion, we'll have to recognize that at times the employed vehicle is a car or other conveyance. All have served bombers' purposes, depending on the size of the explosive load needed for the job. Bicycle bombs were common in Vietnam, with frame tubes and saddlebags packed with explosives. A motorcycle was the delivery vehicle for an attempt against Egyptian Interior Minister Hassan al-Alfi in Cairo in 1993. The explosion, enhanced by ball bearings, killed four bystanders and injured 15, including the Interior Minister.[17]

This building offers better protection against bombing than others shown, because of its small, high windows and parking spaces occupied by employees' vehicles. This isn't absolute protection, because although this building looks like a bunker, it's not as heavily constructed. (Photo by Tony Lesce.)

Truck bombs have, up until now, been seen mainly on foreign shores. This pattern has continued recently. Three months after the World Trade Center bombing, a car bomb killed five in Italy. On October 4 that year, a suicide driver attacked an Israeli bus with a car bomb, injuring 29 people.

1994 also had its allotment of truck and car bombs, and all were abroad. Another car bomb attack against a bus in Israel killed nine people on April 6th. Eleven days later, a car bomb exploded at Johannesburg's airport, injuring 18. On July 18, a car bomb attack against Jewish groups in Buenos Aires, Argentina, killed 95 and injured over 200. Eight days later, a car bomb damaged the Israeli Embassy in London, and another blew up outside a building used by Jewish groups in London. On October 19, a car bomb blew up alongside a bus on Tel Aviv's main street, killing 20 people.

In Algiers, a kamikaze driver directed his car bomb to the police station, where it killed 42 people, on January 30, 1995. The next month, a car bomb killed 94 people when it exploded in a bazaar in Iraq. Not long afterwards, two similar attacks in the Gaza Strip killed one American and seven Israeli soldiers.

Strictly speaking, a wheeled bomb does not have to be on a truck. Car bombs have been in use for years in the Middle East. A horse-drawn wagon was the vehicle an unknown person parked outside the House of Morgan on New York's Wall Street on September 16, 1920, where the TNT it contained killed 35 people and injured hundreds more.

A shopping cart was used as an attack vehicle in Albuquerque, New Mexico, when a man drove it through the glass door of an abortion clinic in February, 1995. With a can of flaming solvent in the basket, the attacker shattered the glass door with the cart, but caused no other destruction.[18]

A point truck bombers sometimes fail to observe is that the vehicle can serve to identify them. One of the men involved in the World Trade Center bombing left a paper trail by renting the vehicle in his own name. The van's Vehicle Identification Number, or VIN, allowed tracing the vehicle back to the rental company. Although the Oklahoma City bomber did not use his real name, the VIN allowed the FBI to trace the vehicle to the rental company and obtain a description.

Renting a truck leaves a paper trail, and even with forged documents, the rental clerk may be able to provide a description. (Photo by Tony Lesce.)

The most terrifying type of truck bomb has been the one piloted by a kamikaze driver intent on earning his heavenly reward in an act of explosive immolation. It's almost impossible to stop a suicide bomber by gunfire, because the bomber is resigned to death, and the vehicle's momentum will drive it forward even if a lucky shot kills the driver outright. One such device destroyed a U.S. Marine garrison in Beirut in 1983, killing about 250 Marines and injuring others. American truck bombers have not been ardent suicide bombers, choosing instead to park their vehicles near a vulnerable spot and walk away after setting a timer.

In Israel, an ominous development is that suicide bombers have now begun dressing like Israeli soldiers. In 1995, two Islamic bombers had donned Israeli soldiers' uniforms to approach their targets without causing alarm, and killed 21 people besides themselves. Another ruse was to wear skullcaps and religious artifacts of the sort used by ultra-religious Jews.[19]

Suicide Bombers

Suicide bombers, both motorized and afoot, have become prominent in the Middle East. Several car bombers pulled up to buses in Israel before detonating themselves, as happened in Afula on April 6, 1994. Several others boarded buses, or walked into crowded places, and blew themselves up. This problem has become so serious in Israel that Israelis have been arresting scores of young Arabs in the hope of preventing some bombings. The arrests began after suicide bomber Ammah Amerneh wrote a testament before donning a bomb and boarding an Israeli bus in Hadera in 1994. The testament urged other Islamic devotees to follow his example.[20]

Suicide bombers have appeared in Northern Ireland, as well, but with a strange twist. Patrick Gillespie was employed as a cook at a Londonderry army base. On October 23, 1990, gunmen invaded his home and took his wife and three children hostage. They strapped him into a car laden with 1,000 pounds of explosives and forced him to drive it into a British army checkpoint, where it exploded.[21]

Are suicide bombers in our future? To date, Americans have not shown much liking for suicide missions. There's no way of predicting accurately if this will change. Now that Middle Eastern terrorists have seen what a happy hunting ground of soft targets they can find in this country, we may see an influx of foreign terrorists willing and eager to give their lives for a cause.

Bombs in the Sky

The bomb that downed a Pan Am 747 over Lockerbie, Scotland, was stunning news, but it wasn't the first bombing of an American carrier. The Arrow Air charter DC-8 bringing American troops home for Christmas in 1985 crashed just after taking off from a refueling stop at Gander, Newfoundland. The Islamic Jihad claimed credit for bringing it down, but the official story was that wing icing had caused the crash. Years later, another view emerged.

It wasn't until 1988 that the Canadian Aviation Safety Board produced a report, split by disagreement. Four of the nine members stated that wing icing was not the cause, and a former Canadian Supreme Court Justice agreed with them. Witnesses had seen the DC-8 in flames before it crashed.

In 1989, the news appeared that Arrow Air had contracted with Lt. Colonel Oliver North to ship arms. The American troops on the flight were on leave from a Sinai peacekeeping mission. Also, over 20 counter-terrorist-trained Special Forces soldiers were on the flight.

Another intriguing aspect was that telephone calls regarding the crash were received by the U.S. Consulate in Oran, Algeria, and by the Reuters wire service in Beirut. The caller to Reuters explained that, as the DC-8 had been delayed for five hours in Cologne, the delay had caused it to explode in Newfoundland instead of over the U.S, as planned. The FBI team investigating the crash was not allowed access to the crash site. These facts suggest that there was a cover-up, possibly to avoid revealing the Iran-Contra connection.[22]

Several years later, it happened again. In December, 1988, a warning that a Pan Am airliner flying from Frankfurt to the United States would be bombed came from an unidentified person to the State Department. The U.S. Embassy in Moscow posted a notice for embassy employees, and the news was sent to American diplomatic offices all over Europe and the Middle East. The news did not reach the general public, however. The unfortunate reason for this is typical of the failure of intelligence work. Many warnings are received, but very few are real. It's simply not possible to react to every warning, especially one from an unknown source.[23]

A favorite trick for placing a bomb aboard an airliner used to be checking in luggage, then not boarding the flight. Today, security procedures require matching all luggage to passengers' names. Airfreight isn't quite as critical, because the bomber doesn't have control over which flight will carry it, or when it departs. Air carriers spot-check airfreight, especially when a shipment isn't from a regular customer.

Recent history shows that placing a bomb aboard an airliner is still possible, despite strict security measures. One attempt that failed because it was so clumsy was when an Arab terrorist gave a calculator containing a bomb to his pregnant Irish fiancée to take with her on a 1986 trip aboard El Al. Other attempts using a dupe have succeeded. Although airport security rent-a-cops ask a person with a portable computer to turn it on to "prove" it's real, a technically adept person can place an explosive charge inside the case without interfering with the computer's operation.

It's not necessary to place a bomb aboard an airliner to do damage. In May, 1995, a pipe bomb detonated in a lavatory in Tokyo's Narita Airport, a striking parallel to the bomb that blew up a baggage locker at New York's LaGuardia Airport 30 years earlier.[24]

Some airports use explosive-sniffing dogs to detect explosives. New technology includes high-tech sensors that can detect the vapors given off by explosives. While technically superb, these methods have their problems. One way of degrading their effectiveness, obvious to a serious terrorist, is to produce a series of false alarms by rubbing a stick of plastic explosive over several pieces of innocent luggage. After several false alarms within a short time, security officers will conclude that something isn't working with the system, or the dog is becoming tired. Another way is to place the explosive in a hermetically sealed container to confine the vapors.

Firebombs

Explosives, although fairly easy to improvise, are not the only route to mass destruction. Until the Oklahoma City bombing, the largest mass murder in American history was the killing of 97 people with a firebomb in the Bronx, New

York, in April, 1990. The perpetrator, Julio Gonzales, put $1 of gasoline into a plastic bottle and threw it through the front door of an after-hours club. With the main exit aflame and the windows barred, most of the people died of smoke inhalation. The few survivors had forced their way through a little-used second door.[25]

The firebomb appears to be a favorite weapon for anti-abortion terrorists, and many abortion clinics have sustained firebomb damage. The Hillcrest Clinic, in Norfolk, Virginia, was damaged by arson in 1983, followed by several pipe bombs in 1984. Although there was extensive damage, nobody was hurt and criminal convictions followed. A shooting in December, 1994, also resulted in no injuries.[26]

Firebombing of abortion clinics continued through the 1980s. A man who had destroyed Cincinnati's Margaret Sanger Clinic on December 30, 1985, received the parole he sought in 1995, under particularly strict conditions. Prosecutors had dropped a charge of firebombing another clinic in exchange for a guilty plea. He had earlier been convicted of firebombing a Pensacola, Florida, abortion clinic.[27]

An abortion clinic in Albuquerque, New Mexico, was the target of a shopping cart fire-bomb attack in early 1995. Another anti-abortion terrorist struck at three abortion clinics in California in a week during February, 1995. Although there was physical damage, and one Planned Parenthood clinic in San Luis Obispo was destroyed, no injuries resulted.[28]

Two more fires occurred in Santa Cruz and San Francisco a few days later. Arson investigators linked the fires because they used flammable liquids in automobile tires. [29] Two road flares on the roof of a Soquel, California, abortion clinic on February 21, 1995 did not cause serious damage.

The New York subway system is extremely vulnerable. A firebomb exploding inside New York's Lexington Avenue Line one block from the World Trade Center in December, 1994, burned 43 people, some critically. It also tied up the system for several hours.[30] Investigation disclosed that the bomb ignited prematurely, injuring the bomber, who had previously placed another subway firebomb that injured two teenagers. He had characterized himself as the "Terror Mad Bomber" in extortion notes found in his home.[31]

Gasoline is an excellent choice for a firebomber. It's commonly available, easily ignited, and easy to carry. A terrorist who throws a bomb containing merely a quart of gasoline into a crowded subway car as the doors close could kill many people. A timer would ignite it as the train leaves the station and begins sliding into the tunnel.

During the crowded rush hour, it's absolutely no problem to board one of New York's Flushing Line trains with two packages and leave one behind when getting off at Grand Central Station, just before the train goes under the river. Physical destruction would be modest, but the lethal effects would be horrific. After 200 people burned to death in a subway car, the result might be a sharp drop in subway riders. People carrying packages would be closely scrutinized, and even attacked. At the very least, there'd be a new panic law prohibiting packages of any kind, even women's handbags, on the subway, but this would be merely a "feel-good" law.

Effective security measures are impractical. Admiral Paul E. Busick, Director of the Office of Intelligence and Security for the U. S. Department of Transportation, stated that "... there's no technological fix. It's not like you can put in a bunch of metal detectors and bomb detectors and be able to run the number of people through a transit system that go through it daily." He went on to point out that a new and relatively small system is easier to secure, using many police officers and cameras, than a large, widespread and old system, such as New York's.[32] Of course, security wouldn't stop the serious bomber. A terrorist could easily carry gasoline in plastic bags under his coat during the cold season.

Even if subways became difficult targets because of closely controlled security checkpoints, movie theaters would provide soft targets. Again, a likely agent would be gasoline, because of its availability. A seven day waiting period for each gasoline purchase is unimaginable. Any concert hall, theater, auditorium, church, supermarket, or even a gay bar is a potential target. A terrorist would only have to toss in a fire bomb. If loss of life was the intent, it wouldn't take much to block the exits.

Gasoline is versatile. Used in liquid form, it's excellent for fire-bombing, even without additives. With an additive to make it sticky, the firebomber produces "napalm," an incendiary substance that sticks to what it touches.

Because of the sensitivity of modern high-technology equipment, such as computers, to heat, firebombing is as effective as using explosives. A few gallons of gasoline would be just as effective as high explosives in destroying a modern telephone switching system.

Historically, gasoline has been far more effective than explosives in lethality. It took about two tons of improvised ammonium nitrate and fuel oil to produce the Oklahoma City blast that killed 168 people. Less than a gallon of gasoline produced the Bronx fire that killed 97.

In vapor form, gasoline is a highly effective low explosive. Inside a structure, the effect is devastating on both people and equipment. By blocking exits, a determined terrorist can ensure that there are no survivors.

Fuzing Systems

Perhaps the most important feature of a terrorist bomb is the delayed-action fuze, which allows the person who plants the bomb to be far away when it detonates. Another advantage of the fuze is that it allows selective bombing, important because by its very nature a bomb is indiscriminate. Precise timing allows detonation when the target is within the lethal radius.

A "fuze" is the correct term for the device that triggers the bomb, unlike a "fuse," which is an electrical device that melts and interrupts the current when the load exceeds the fuse's rating. Fuzes come in several types: flame, mechanical, electrical, time, chemical, and improvised. The military uses all types of fuzes, and some military commando units receive training in making improvised fuzes when manufactured ones are not available.

A flame fuze is a chemically treated cord that burns with an intense flame at a given rate when lit, until the flame reaches the blasting cap and sets off the bomb. The main disadvantage of a flame fuze is that it burns quickly, allowing little time for getting away from the blast. Another problem is that it's conspicuous, because the flame is very visible.

A mechanical fuze is a device that releases a firing pin or striker to detonate a primer, which in turn ignites a booster charge that sets off the bomb. The striker can be released by pressure or release of pressure. A land mine uses a pressure release device. A string or trip wire stretched across a corridor releases the striker when broken. A barometric fuze detonates the bomb at a certain altitude, and is designed for destruction of airliners when terrorists don't know the precise schedule.

The electrical fuze uses electric current to trigger the blasting cap and detonate the bomb. The electricity can come from a battery or from house current. A bomb wired to an electric light switch detonates when someone turns on the lights. A bomb inside a telephone explodes when someone picks up the telephone.

A type of electrical fuze is used for the lay-off bomb, a heavy charge planted under a road or by a roadside, detonating when the target vehicle is adjacent to the bomb. Spain's Admiral Luis Carrero Blanco was killed with this type of bomb in Madrid in 1973.

A radio-controlled fuze is also electrical. One such was the device an Israeli hit team used to assassinate an Arab leader in Paris in 1972 in reprisal for the Munich massacre. One Israeli operative telephoned the target from a phone booth near his home, and when he heard the target's voice, he pressed the button on his radio transmitter, detonating the charge inside the earpiece.

Another type of electrical fuze is the time-delay fuze, which can use a mechanical clock, wired so that when one of the hands reaches a certain point, it contacts a wire to complete the circuit. More versatile is the timer using an electronic watch, or the timer inside a videotape recorder, which can be programmed for weeks in advance. Removing the tape transport mechanism and amplifier frees space for explosives, and the VCR then becomes a long-delay time-bomb.

A quartz-watch timer was used in the attempt on Britain's Prime Minister, Margaret Thatcher, when she attended a Conservative Party Conference in Brighton in 1984. The bomber took Room 629 in the Grand Hotel, five floors above the room allotted for Thatcher, and hid about 11 kilograms of high explosive behind a panel in the bathroom. During the following weeks, other guests used the room, until 2:54 on the morning of October 12, when it devastated the hotel. The blast traveled downward, destroying Thatcher's bathroom underneath. By luck, Thatcher had left her bathroom just a few minutes before the blast, and was unharmed. Five British politicians were killed, and 30 injured.[33]

At times, life imitates art. In 1974, Stein and Day published Donald Seaman's novel, *The Bomb That Could Lip-Read*, describing a plot by the IRA to bomb a high-level conference using a sophisticated electronic timer to detonate the bomb. It's impossible to tell at this time whether the perpetrators of the Brighton bombing had gotten any ideas by reading this book.

The electronic time-delay and radio-controlled fuzes allow precision in targeting. Selective bombing killed Britain's Lord Louis Mountbatten and his boating party on August 8, 1979, when they were at sea off the Irish coast. A time-delay bomb allows destruction of an airliner over water, assuring 100 percent fatalities and burial of the evidence at sea. A time-delay fuze detonated a bomb inside an Air India flight off the coast of Ireland in 1985, and the resulting crash killed all 329 people aboard.

A barometric fuze is designed to ignite the bomb when air pressure drops to a certain point. This is the type of fuze some bombers use against airliners. The fuze triggers the device when the aircraft reaches a certain altitude. One example was the device the Unabomber placed aboard an American Airlines flight in 1979, which set off an incendiary bomb in the cargo hold. Although some passengers suffered from smoke inhalation, there were no deaths, and the aircraft landed safely.

The most sophisticated devices to date for use against aircraft combine quartz timers and barometric fuzes. These are for use when the airliner makes intermediate stops, and are to ensure that the barometric fuze does not become active until the airliner is over water. Some terrorists, knowing that evidence from the crash can lead to them, prefer that the airliner blow up over the ocean, where recovery of crash fragments is extremely difficult.

At times, this doesn't work, because departure is delayed. Pan Am Flight 103 left London's Heathrow Airport 25 minutes later than scheduled, and was still over land when the bomb exploded.[34]

The chemical fuze uses acid to eat through a barrier. The thickness of the barrier determines the delay, and when the acid penetrates, it dissolves a wire holding the striker, which a spring then drives forward to set off the bomb. Chemical fuzes are difficult to manufacture and are less precise and reliable than other types, especially the quartz timer.

Information on a variety of bombs and fuzing systems is commonly available in books by many publishers. One survey of terrorist organizations has a comprehensive chapter on bombs and fuzes.[35] Designs range from sophisticated manufactured fuzes to simple, improvised models.

Improvised fuzes can be crude or extremely sophisticated, depending on the judgment and skill of the bomb's builder.

The clothespin and wedge pull fuze is so well-known it requires no discussion here. A much more sophisticated improvised fuze is an adaptation of a model airplane radio-control device. Instead of actuating the model airplane's control surfaces, the receiver provides the current to detonate a blasting cap. The transmitter can be hundreds of yards away, or even farther if the bomber uses a special amplifier.

Terrorist bombers also use anti-tamper devices to kill any bomb squad officer trying to disarm the device. There are as many types of anti-tamper devices and switches as there are types of bombs. One used heavy black photographic packaging paper to shield a photoelectric cell. Removing the wrapping would allow light into the package, setting off the fuze.[36]

Inventive bomb builders will often use two detonating switches, calculating that if a bomb disposal officer deactivates one, the other will get him. Others use mercury switches, the kind found in thermostats, to prevent moving the bomb. Once activated, any slight rocking motion makes the mercury flow and completes the circuit.

Because of their design, blasting caps have a serious weakness which authorities exploit. The blasting cap contains a small amount of extremely sensitive explosive called "priming compound," with a fine wire embedded in it. Passing a small amount of electricity through the wire causes it to become very hot, igniting the primer. These fine wires are sensitive to electromagnetic radiation, which can induce enough current in them to ignite the primer. This is why we see signs urging motorists and others to turn off radio transmitters at construction sites.

The countermeasure is a wide-band radio transmitter that puts out pulses on many frequencies, on the principle that one frequency will be that to which the blasting cap's wiring is "tuned," so that the pulse will induce a current in the wire. This will cause a premature detonation, sometimes even killing the bomber if he's still carrying the bomb.

Bomb Threats

These are today a fact of life, a risk-free way for someone angry at the world, or with another cause, to produce fear and disruption. Some school-age pranksters call in bomb threats because they know these often result in evacuation of the school and an afternoon's diversion. In some companies, employees call in bomb threats to get an afternoon off or to break up the monotony.

Callers also tend to follow news events. During the build-up to the Gulf War in 1991, 461 bomb threats were reported in New York City in less than 48 hours.[37]

One silly and trivial example, which had serious results for the caller, was a traveler's spurious bomb threat, sent in via his cellular phone, as he was driving to the Rome airport. This passenger was late for his flight, and wanted it held up for a few minutes. The Caracas-bound flight was actually held up for 35 minutes, but when it left, the passenger wasn't on it. Police had traced the call to his cellular phone and arrested him when he checked in.[38]

A particularly sinister type of bomb threat is that directed against a hospital. While other types of buildings can be easily evacuated, hospitals cannot, without risk to many patients. One sidelight of the Oklahoma City bombing was a flurry of telephoned bomb threats against hospitals, both in Oklahoma City and around the country.

A bomb threat isn't necessarily a prank. A professional terrorist may place a dummy bomb on the premises and call in a threat as a form of reconnaissance, to determine how well security responds. This dry run serves as a dress rehearsal for the real event later.[39]

A bomb threat can also be a tactical move to facilitate another type of action. When members of the Silent Brotherhood decided to rob a bank in Spokane, Washington in 1984, they first planted a realistic dummy bomb at a clothing store several miles from the bank. They then phoned the store to report the bomb before entering the bank, thereby drawing police units to the store and leaving them a free hand to rob the bank.[40]

More Bombs to Come

As for future bombings, these are virtually certain. One trend which has disturbed law enforcement officers is the profusion of bomb-making information available through open sources. There is a virtual bibliography of bomb-making books put out by various publishers and available by mail order and in some bookstores. Bomb-making information is available via modem, as well. As of 1995, there were more than 300 books on bombs currently in print in the U.S. including *The Blaster's Handbook*, published by the United States Department of Agriculture (Forest Service). The *Encyclopaedia Brittanica* also dispenses learned information on bomb components under the "explosives" category. By 1992, there had been at least 12 incidents in which the bomb-making information came from home computer bulletin boards.[41] The trend has accelerated, and today bomb-making information is available on the Internet.

The government can't guard every installation equally. The White House is protected, but federal buildings across the country are vulnerable and will remain vulnerable despite a few stop-gap measures such as concrete barriers and superannuated "security guards." As for car bombings, an airport or parking garage is a perfect place for them, because of traffic density.

This may also happen in New York. Once, when traffic was much lighter and parking easier, car bombings were more frequent, as we've already noted. However, trying to find a parking place downtown is harder these days. Only a few buildings, such as the World Trade Center, have their own underground parking garages. This doesn't preclude someone double-parking on one of New York's crowded streets, locking the vehicle, and ducking down a subway stair to escape. A member of the Japanese Red Army was arrested in New Jersey in 1988, transporting bombs intended for office buildings in downtown Manhattan. [42] Overall, though, it's much, much easier to find a downtown parking space in Oklahoma City, Phoenix, or Albuquerque.

We can learn a lot about bombers, their techniques, and the law enforcement response by studying one long-term case, the "Unabomber," who has eluded the FBI for nearly two decades.

Notes:

1. Clark, Jacob R., "Crime in the 90's: It's a Blast," *Law Enforcement News*, March 15, 1994, p. 1.
2. Richardson, Allen F., "Bomb Kills Lawmaker in Britain," *USA Today*, July 31, 1990, p. 4.
3. Lacayo, Richard, "To the Bench Via the Chair," *Time*, September 14, 1992, p. 41.
4. Clark, Jacob R., "Crime in the 90's: It's a Blast," *Law Enforcement News*, March 15, 1994, p. 1.
5. *Counterbomb*, Myers, Lawrence W., Boulder, CO, Paladin Press, 1991, pp. 2-3.
6. Lee, Edward L., "Violent Avengers," *Security Management*, v33 n12, December, 1989, p. 38.
7. Morris, Julie, and Mayfield, Mark, "Mail Bomb Sent to TV Preacher," *USA Today*, January 31, 1991, p. 3A.
8. Rota, Kelly, "Explosive in Bombs Identified; FBI: 'We're Making Some Progress,'" *USA Today*, January 3, 1991, p. 3A.
9. Johnson, Kevin, "Family's 'Real Life' Racism; Whites are Divided Over Black Neighbors," *USA Today*, March 13, 1992, p. 3A.
10. Associated Press, March 29, 1994.

11. Johnson, Kevin, "Fifth Bomb Explodes in Indiana," *USA Today*, January 6, 1992, p. 3A.
12. Meddis, Sam Vincent, "FBI Checks 'Amateurish' Pipe Bombs," *USA Today*, February 5, 1991, p. 1A.
13. Harney, James, "FBI Hasn't Linked Bombs to Terrorists," *USA Today*, February 6, 1991, p. 4A.
14. Associated Press, May 3, 1995.
15. Clark, Jacob R., "Crime in the 90's: It's a Blast," *Law Enforcement News*, March 15, 1994, p. 7.
16. Ellis, David, "The Hit Man Plays a Deadly Tune," *Time*, May 4, 1991, p. 17.
17. Nelan, Bruce W., "Bombs in the Name of Allah," *Time*, August 30, 1993, p. 28.
18. Pells, Eddie, "Abortion Clinic: Man Charged in Four Instances," Associated Press, February 24, 1995.
19. "Israel: Suicide Bombers Dressed Like Israeli Soldiers to Avoid Detection," Associated Press, February 2, 1995.
20. Abu-Nasr, Donna, "Israel Targets Young Militants to Thwart Suicide Attacks," Associated Press, April 15, 1994.
21. Phillips, Andrew, "'Human Bombs': The IRA Uses A Chilling Tactic of Terrorism," *Maclean's*, v103, n45, November 5, 1990, p. 38.
22. Rowan, Roy, "Gander: Different Crash, Same Questions," *Time*, April 27, 1992, p. 33.
23. "Terror in The Night," *Time*, January 2, 1989, p. 74.
24. Reid, T. R., "Pipe Bomb Rips Tokyo Airport," *Washington Post*, May 14, 1995, p. A20.
25. Magnuson, Ed, "The Devil Made Him Do It," *Time*, April 9, 1990, p. 38.
26. Taylor, Joe, "Clinic Shooting: Clinic Shot up by Gunman Has History of Protests, Violence," Associated Press, January 1, 1995.
27. Sniffen, Michael J., "Abortion Clinic Bomber Put Under Strict Parole Conditions," Associated Press, January 17, 1995.

28. "Abortion Clinic Fire: Suspected Arson Hits Third Clinic in Week,"Associated Press, February 15, 1995.

29. Cole, Richard, "Abortion Clinic Fires: San Francisco Clinic Latest Target," Associated Press, February 28, 1995.

30. Hampson, Rick, "Progress Offers Up Tools of Terrorism," Associated Press, March 21, 1995. Hays, Tom, "Subway Fire-bombing: Fire-bomb Rips Subway Car, Injures 43," Associated Press, December 24, 1994.

31. Hays, Tom, "Subway Fire-bombing: Suspect's Note Says 'Terror Mad Bomber,'" Associated Press, December 23, 1994.

32. "Subway Security: Security Expert Says Incidents Like NY Subway Blast Hard to Prevent," Associated Press, December 21, 1994.

33. *Braver Men Walk Away*, Gurney, Peter, London, HarperCollins Publishers, 1993, p. 171.

34. "Diabolically Well-Planned," *Time*, January 9, 1989, p. 26.

35. *Terrorist Organizations in the United States*, Mullin, Wayman C., Springfield, IL, Charles C. Thomas, Publisher, 1988, pp. 123-140.

36. *Braver Men Walk Away*, Gurney, Peter, London, HarperCollins Publishers, 1993, p. 158.

37. Squitieri, Tom, "Security: The Word of the Hour," *USA Today*, January 19, 1991, p. 9A.

38. Associated Press, May 5, 1995.

39. *Counterbomb*, Myers, Lawrence W., Boulder, CO, Paladin Press, 1991, p. 21.

40. *The Silent Brotherhood*, Flynn, Kevin, and Gerhardt, Gary, New York, The Free Press, 1989, p 130.

41. Clark, Jacob R., "Crime in the 90's: It's a Blast," *Law Enforcement News*, March 15, 1994, p. 7.

42. *Terrorism*, Holms, John Pynchon, and Burke, Tom, New York, Pinnacle Books, 1994, p. 216.

Chapter Seven
Case Study:
The Unabomber

Unabomber sketch circulated by the F.B.I.

A notorious and mysterious bomber has been sending bombs to various people and agencies since 1978. Some have traveled through the mail, while others have been aboard airliners. Bombs credited to him totaled 16 by April, 1995, and his career has lasted longer than New York's notorious Mad

Bomber. The FBI has dubbed him the "Unabomber" (alternate spelling: "Unabomer") because many of his targets were universities and people who worked for them, while other targets have been the President of United Airlines and the Boeing Company. In 1979, an incendiary bomb attributed to the Unabomber detonated in the baggage hold of American Airlines Flight 444, before landing at Dulles International Airport. The FBI has not disclosed whether this bomb was in a piece of check-in luggage or in a package sent through the U.S. Postal Service.

In 1987, another bomb placed near a computer store in Salt Lake City, Utah, exploded when the owner kicked it. For six years after that, the Unabomber was dormant, but apparently roused himself in July, 1993, with a package bomb that injured a University of California professor. A second bomb, sent within days, injured a Yale University professor.

To date, the Unabomber has racked up three fatalities. The first was a computer store owner in Sacramento, California, in December, 1985, killed by a bomb in a paper bag left behind his store. This may have been inadvertent, because the other fatalities had packages addressed to them or their organizations. The second was an advertising executive killed by a bomb sent to his residence on December 10, 1994. The third was a timber industry lobbyist who opened a package on April 24, 1995, which was addressed to his predecessor.

Characteristics of the Unabomber's products have been few and inconsistent. Some bombs were in paper bags, while others were in wooden boxes. Several sent through the mail were in cardboard boxes. The Unabomber has used no electronic components, according to information released by the FBI, as these would have helped trace him. His only identifying mark has been the initials "FC" scribed on metal components that survived the blasts. A few letters he sent to newspapers and magazines contained the claim that he was part of a group, although the FBI still believes he is acting alone.[1]

During late June, 1995, the Unabomber sent a letter to the *San Francisco Chronicle* threatening to blow up an airliner at Los Angeles International Airport, causing widespread concern throughout California. A later letter, to *The New York Times*, stated that this threat had been merely a "prank."[2]

A characteristic of the Unabomber's letters is that they refer to "we," as if written by a spokesman for a group. Law enforcement authorities seem to think that the Unabomber is only one man, based on descriptions of a person seen near the site of a bombing. However, this can only be speculative unless and until they catch the perpetrator(s). The tone and language of the letters released so far suggest that the Unabomber is a Luddite, because of his anti-industrial views.

The FBI, the Bureau of Alcohol, Tobacco, and Firearms (BATF), and the Postal Inspectors have formulated a "best guess" profile of the Unabomber. According to this description, he is a white male in his late 40s or early 50s, "obsessive-compulsive," and has difficulties forming personal relationships. He is probably neat and rigid, with a macabre sense of humor, and not apparently predisposed to violence.[3]

The FBI places great stock in its Behavioral Sciences Unit, which has developed profiles of serial killers and rapists. In certain cases, it has used psychological techniques against suspects to induce confessions.

One tactic the FBI appears to be using is taunting the Unabomber into making a mistake that would help identify him. A 1995 *Newsweek* article contains disparaging statements about him by FBI spokesmen, calling him "vain," "windy," and "grandiose." Tom Strentz, an FBI agent, stated that the Unabomber is now in competition with the Oklahoma City bombers, and is afraid of being "upstaged."

The most "promising" feature, according to the FBI, is that he is now allegedly taking more serious risks since Oklahoma. This implies the uncomfortable question of how many more people will die or be injured while the Unabomber is trying to gain notoriety, and questions the wisdom of taunting him to greater efforts. At the same time, FBI technicians are poring over the Unabomber's letters to try to trace the paper, ink, and other characteristics that might bring them closer to establishing his identity.

Meanwhile, the Unabomber said that his threat against an airliner flying out of Los Angeles International Airport had been "one last prank," suggesting that he might be retiring. If so, the chances of the FBI apprehending him will become extremely remote. He has made threats, though, stating that if the manifesto he sent to several newspapers and magazines isn't published, or if it appears in *Penthouse* first, he will detonate at least one more bomb. Only time will tell.

Notes:

1. Morganthau, Tom, Carroll, Ginny, Liu, Melinda, and Bogert, Carroll, "Who Is He?" *Newsweek*, May 8, 1995, pp. 40-41.
2. Lambropoulos, Dino, "Unabomber Says Threat A 'Prank,'" Associated Press, June 29, 1995.
3. "What Makes Bombers Tick?," *Law Enforcement News*, March 15, 1994, p. 7.

Chapter Eight
The Nuclear Threat

Ten or more years ago, there was a lot of concern over the prospects of terrorists stealing a nuclear bomb, or obtaining the material for making one. While there had been reason for concern since the dawn of the nuclear age, given the inconsistent safeguards, this threat has not materialized. There have been occasional threats to detonate a nuclear bomb, and the government has had to take them seriously. All turned out to be unfounded. A report that President Gerald Ford had come within ten minutes of ordering the evacuation of Boston in 1975 appears to have been merely a rumor.[1]

There exist guidelines regarding whether or not the government should take a nuclear threat seriously. While these are classified, it's easy to calculate that they include:

A threat from someone known to have the knowledge, propensity, and materials for carrying out his threat.

A threat shortly after theft of nuclear materials.

A threat accompanied by a demonstration, such as a nuclear explosion in a remote area.[2]

The federal government has, since 1975, maintained a special response unit in Nevada, known as the Nuclear Emergency Search Team (NEST), to search for nuclear devices. With its fleet of aircraft and sensitive detectors, the team would scan the site of a threat and try to find the bomb before detonation.

The "secret" of building a nuclear bomb hasn't been secret for a long time. Published information, such as the *Los Alamos*

Handbook, provides enough information for someone with a suitable background to design a bomb. One U.S. Government report stated that it would be possible, using only reactor-grade fissile materials, to construct a reliable nuclear bomb in the kiloton range.[3] It might not be elegant, or even efficient, but it would probably work.

The overwhelming fact, though, is that even if a bomb did not yield a nuclear explosion, the aftereffects would be extremely destructive. A "fizzle yield" would scatter radioactive material, and its effects would depend on the exact site of the detonation. One exploding in a basement would not scatter as much as one detonating on the top floor of a skyscraper.

It's easy to see that it's not necessary for a terrorist to know how to build a nuclear bomb to set off an explosion that would suit his purpose. Contaminating midtown Manhattan or the Wall Street area with radioactive debris by setting off a conventional explosive to disperse radioactive dust could kill thousands of people, and make the area unsafe until it was decontaminated.

Nuclear Bluff

An opportunistic terrorist with no access to nuclear materials could still cause serious disruption by coat-tailing, delivering a threat on the heels of a theft of nuclear materials. This is a good reason for suspecting that, if nuclear thefts have occurred, they've been kept top secret. However, it may not be possible to keep all nuclear thefts secret. A hijacking of Department of Energy nuclear couriers on a public road would attract media attention, and would open the way to a nuclear bluff. It would then be very difficult to differentiate between a bluff and a genuine threat by the possessors of the nuclear material.

Nuclear Theft

There have been thefts of nuclear material. During the last few years, Western European police have caught several people trying to smuggle nuclear material from Russia into Europe. With the situation in the former Soviet Union unstable and deteriorating, there are ample opportunities for theft, although nobody appears to have purloined a bomb or missile yet.

Complicating the picture is the problem of "MUF," Material Unaccounted For. This is shrinkage of stockpiles during processing, resulting from leaks, spills, and other innocent causes. It's the fact that shrinkage is difficult to measure and control which sets up the possibility of theft by stealth. This sort of theft would have to be an "inside" job, with employees of nuclear establishments making off with small quantities and escaping detection.

There are at least two reasons for stealing nuclear materials: For use or for sale. An opportunistic criminal gang might find it lucrative to sell fissile material to a well-funded terrorist group that lacks local resources to engineer the theft itself.

According to some authoritative sources, stealing nuclear material isn't terribly difficult.[4] In the United States, the departments of Energy and Defense keep nuclear materials under guard, but the level of security varies.

Military facilities are very closely guarded, because they store active nuclear bombs. Nuclear processing plants are less closely guarded, and nuclear power generating plants depend on private security guards of varying quality. Two newspaper reporters were able to penetrate the Palo Verde Nuclear Generating Station west of Phoenix, Arizona, a few years ago, without being challenged by guards.[5]

This should not be surprising. Guard forces for these plants are mostly private security, or rent-a-cops. Their training is insufficient, and it's almost certain that they would not be able to handle a serious threat. Private guard forces are adequate for patrolling fence lines and manning security gates. They are effective in keeping out drunks, and making a show of security.

Although armed and authorized to use deadly force under specified circumstances, nuclear plant guard forces and their managers face the prospect of liability. An unjustified shooting has serious repercussions, and these guards would be extremely reluctant to open fire. This reluctance provides a terrorist attacker with a valuable edge.

Getting into a plant undetected is one thing. Getting out with a significant amount of nuclear material is another. Even a penetration is significant, because it means that a terrorist would be able to effect entry, carry out a reconnaissance, and return later with a raiding party to carry out the theft.

Terrorists might decide not to attempt theft, because of the need to get away safely with the stolen material. Instead, sabotage is an alternative, using either explosives or arson to damage the nuclear reactors and their control rooms. Depending on the extent of the damage, a nuclear power plant could become inoperative for years.

A weak point in the nuclear materials handling system is transportation, when the bombs or raw materials leave the safety of fixed and guarded installations and go on the road. The Department of Energy operates a Transportation Safeguards Division (TSD), to protect high-security shipments. TSD headquarters is in Albuquerque, New Mexico, and other courier operations centers are at Oak Ridge, Tennessee, and Amarillo, Texas. A nuclear separation plant is at Oak Ridge, and the Pantex bomb manufacturing plant is near Amarillo.

The TSD employs 282 nuclear couriers, or guards, and operates a fleet of special high-security tractor-trailer trucks and escort vehicles. The vehicles are unmarked, but have U.S. government license plates, and their schedules are classified to avoid giving free information to potential ambushers. Tractors are armored, and the couriers carry an array of small arms with them. They also have berths, allowing the truck to travel nonstop. Driving is limited to 32 hours of continuous travel, to allow crews rest stops.

The nuclear material is in a special locked "Safe Secure Trailer," designed to protect the cargo in case of an accident, with a special tie-down system. An additional safety precaution is that convoys do not exceed 55 miles per hour.

Escort vehicles are Ford vans and Chevrolet Suburbans, designed to carry crews of armed guards to support the driver and crew of the tractor-trailer in case of ambush. Couriers are trained to handle attacks, and regularly take refresher training. Convoys are in constant radio contact with headquarters (known as SECOM) in Albuquerque, and SECOM has telephone numbers for state police dispatch in all states. This allows a convoy to call for help from state and local police if necessary. The emphasis is on obtaining reinforcements from police to repel an attack.

Despite the constant radio communication with head-quarters, convoys are still vulnerable to ambush. Away from home, they have only their own resources, and a well-equipped ierrorist group could ambush a convoy. It would help to obtain inside information regarding schedules, but observation would tell terrorists the precise moment a convoy began a trip. The length of each road trip, lengthened by the self-imposed 55 mph limit, would make it easier to set up an ambush.

The TSD does not publicly discuss its practices, but prudent convoy procedure is to have a pilot vehicle drive hundreds of yards ahead of the main convoy in order to report problems on the road ahead by radio. This makes it harder to stage a road "accident" to stop the convoy. However, resourceful terrorists would have little trouble identifying the pilot vehicle and putting it discreetly out of action. A terrorist group with heavy weapons, such as man-portable rocket launchers, would be able to neutralize the crews of the tractor and escort vehicles very quickly.

It's reasonable that a radio tracking transmitter would be in each vehicle to enable SECOM to maintain moment to moment location of each vehicle. It's also reasonable to expect that anti-theft devices would be on the Safe Secure trailer. These probably include booby-traps releasing tear gas or other noxious substances in case of unauthorized entry, and time-delay locks on the inner container. The purpose is to delay access to the nuclear material until reinforcements can arrive.

The success of such an ambush depends on getting away before any police elements arrive. Given the vast distances in the Western United States, where most of these convoys operate, driving time for reinforcements, even if a radio call gets through, would prevent their immediate arrival.

Given the amounts of nuclear materials in the rest of the world, it's unlikely that an ambush on a TSD convoy will take place in the near future. Should the situation change, and terrorists become bolder or more desperate, this could well happen.

Notes:

1. *Disruptive Terrorism*, Santoro, Victor, Port Townsend, WA, Loompanics Unlimited, 1984, p. 49.
2. *Ibid.*, p. 50.
3. Beres, Louis Rene, *International Terrorism*, Kegley, Charles W., Editor, NY, St. Martin's Press, 1990, p. 230.
4. *Technological Terrorism*, Clark, Richard C., Old Greenwich, CT, Devin-Adair Company, 1980, pp. 7-66.
5. *Arizona Republic*, April 15, 1984.

Chapter Nine
Chemical and Biological Threats

The United States, with its large population centers, offers a rich array of vulnerable points for chemical or biological terrorism. Spraying nerve gas in an empty field is pointless. A crowded theater or department store, however, is a very productive target.

Chemical Threats

The 1995 nerve gas attack on the Tokyo subway system was widely publicized, and one question the media did not address was why this hadn't happened in one of the United States' vulnerable public transport systems. The New York subway system, for example, is so unguarded that some passengers even urinate and defecate freely in the stations and passageways. By contrast, Washington DC's Metro is heavily policed, and anyone even eating food or candy is likely to be accosted by a police officer.

Some fears are totally groundless. Poisoning a city's water supply would take a huge amount of a chemical agent. Let's assume a poison with a lethal dose of half a gram. Assume this dose dissolved in eight ounces of water, a practical amount. This calculates to eight grams per gallon. A medium size city consumes about 40 million gallons per day.

Even allowing that most of that would be wasted washing cars, watering lawns, etc., it would still be necessary to poison the entire amount, because it's impossible to know which eight ounces will find their way into a water glass. It works out to 320,000 kilograms needed to poison the entire 40 million gallons. How many trucks or freight cars does it take to haul that? That's 352 English tons.

This is a far cry from a terrorist gaining access to a water supply by crawling under a fence, removing a small vial from an inside pocket, and emptying it into the reservoir. You'd have to lay tracks to the reservoir and drive in a freight train.

There is an exception. Some chemical plants are located near waterways, and spills have occurred by accident. When seventy tons of carbon tetrachloride accidentally spilled into the Ohio River, it caused widespread contamination. [1]

Non-Lethal Chemical Attacks

There have been a few relatively harmless chemical attacks on public places in the United States. These were more malicious pranks than lethal attacks because of the agents employed.

An early example was the release of tear gas on a bridge in San Francisco in 1976, which affected drivers and resulted in stalled traffic. [2]

In 1983, a client in jeans and a camouflage jacket dropped a military tear gas grenade in a Phoenix bar catering to homosexuals. The gas quickly caused patrons to head for the nearest exits.

Pepper spray, used by police officers as a defensive tool, causes choking, closing of the eyes, and collapse when sprayed into the face. When dispersed in the air, it has no identifiable odor, but causes persistent coughing. In 1992, customers in a Mesa, Arizona, supermarket were victims of pepper spray, either discharged into an air-conditioning intake or sprayed into the air and allowed to disperse. The entire store was evacuated while the Mesa Fire Department set up large fans to clear the air.

Stink bombs are very effective in a place of business. During 1994, anti-abortion activists used butyric acid to pollute the air in two abortion clinics in upper New York State. The foul-smelling chemical made over three dozen people ill, and caused more than $50,000 of damage at the clinics. [3]

The Silent Killers

To date, there have been no biological attacks by terrorists. We can expect some efforts in the future, not because terrorists might steal closely guarded military supplies, but because they might grow their own.

Biological agents are weapons of mass destruction, but unlike nuclear weapons, they don't produce a radioactive signature that a search team can detect from afar. An accident can release a biological agent during manufacture, storage, or transportation, but the appearance of a new disease doesn't automatically put anti-terrorist teams on alert.

Biological agents have made poor war weapons, not because they're outlawed by international agreements, but because they're indiscriminate, respecting no frontiers. A biological agent used against an enemy would probably spread to neighboring nations, and even come back to the country that dispersed it. This isn't necessarily a disadvantage to a terrorist, especially one who expects to die during his mission. The suicide bomber mentality can work as well with a silent biological killer.

Unlike chemical agents, biological agents don't disperse and become ineffective with time. Biological agents reproduce, and some form spores under unfavorable conditions. Spores can revive when a suitable target ingests them. Guinard Island, off Britain's coast, was a testing ground for an anthrax weapon during WWII. The agent still lingers on the island, which is why visitors are banned.

Theoretically, it's possible to develop a biological agent to contaminate a water supply. The agent would have to be resistant to aeration, ultraviolet light, and chlorination, as well as being highly infectious. In practice, a terrorist would be better off developing an aerosol, such as pneumonic plague. To a terrorist, an airport is a perfect dispersal point, because travelers would spread the disease over a wide area. A terrorist, carrying the agent in a pressure can disguised as air freshener or shaving cream, could easily spray the lethal agent into the air. It wouldn't even be necessary to pass any security checkpoint, because the terminal's air-conditioning system would quickly recirculate the contaminated air and disperse the agent all over the building.

To date, there have been a couple of abortive efforts to manufacture biological agents which have come to light. In Columbus, Ohio, a man who was alleged to be a white supremacist was arrested in 1995 for illegally procuring bubonic plague bacteria through the mail. Police stated that he had bought $300 of *Yersina Pestis* by falsely claiming that he was a laboratory. Unfortunately for him, he was indiscreet in making statements to fellow employees about his radical views.[4]

In Tokyo, the Aum Shinri Kyo cult accused of the sarin attack against the subway system in 1995 was discovered to have an interest in the Ebola virus. A radio program by this group discussed the use of biological weapons in an apocalyptic war.[5]

The Aum Shinri Kyo cult also downloaded a U.S. government-funded data bank maintained by the Brookhaven National Laboratory in New York, which contained detailed information about the deadly toxins in snake venom, as well as other biological molecules and substances of potential interest to terrorists.[6]

For terrorists' purposes, it wouldn't even be necessary to develop a new lethal agent to cause mass illness and disruption. Coccidioidomycosis, commonly known as "desert fever," is a common fungus in the American Southwest. Normally dormant in the sand, the spore becomes active when a strong wind brings it up into the air and into someone's lungs. Symptoms are fever and weakness, and the fever is highly infectious. Despite its low mortality rate, desert fever makes a good biological weapon because of the potentially large number of victims.[7] With a large percentage of an area's population sick, the economic losses would be astronomical because most business would come to a halt, and federal aid would become necessary. Even a few days' illness overtaking the majority of an area's residents would be a major disaster. This would be a disruption, and we'll examine disruption more closely in the next chapter.

A Greater Threat

From a terrorist's perspective, chemical and biological agents are easier to manufacture or procure than nuclear materials. Harder to detect, they pose more of a threat than most favored weapons of mass destruction.

Notes:

1. *Technological Terrorism*, Clark, Richard C., Old Greenwich, CT, Devin-Adair Company, 1980, p. 114.
2. *Ibid.*, p. 117.
3. "Abortion Clinic: Two Sentenced for Acid-Dumping," Associated Press, February 2, 1995.
4. Associated Press, May 17, 1995.
5. Associated Press, May 24, 1995
6. Royce, Knut, "Was U.S. Technology Used in Subway Attack?", *The Sunday Oregonian*, October 1, 1995, p. 15A.

7. *Disruptive Terrorism*, Santoro, Victor, Port Townsend, WA, Loompanics Unlimited, 1984, p. 77.

Chapter Ten
Disruption

It doesn't take much to bring our highly organized 20th century industrial society to a standstill. One look at a freeway after an accident shows how little it takes to paralyze road traffic. This obvious vulnerability led to the threat of "stall-ins" at the time of the 1964 New York World's Fair. It was a credible threat, and carrying it out would have paralyzed New York City's road network. Fortunately, the civil-rights groups menacing New York with this threat got cold feet at the last minute.

Sabotage

Sabotage is a form of disruption, often involving much less damage than total destruction. Sabotage is striking at a key point to paralyze the entire system. Cutting a power line can be as effective as blowing up the generating plant, blacking out an area without the loss of life caused by an explosion.

A congressional researcher told the Senate Government Affairs Committee that a sniper "could destroy enough facilities to cause a short-term blackout over a metropolitan area." Rifle fire would fray or cut high-tension cables, and although repair is quick, the widespread vulnerability of power lines means that a rifle-equipped terrorist would be able to cut the wires at other points even before repairs were completed.[1]

Environmental Groups

Certain groups, such as Earth First!, publish newsletters and books describing ways to sabotage heavy equipment to prevent destruction of forest lands. One book, *EcoDefense*, contains many technical descriptions of how to sabotage earth-moving equipment, aircraft, and traplines. It also contains descriptions and diagrams of how to set spikes into a road to deny it to logging and earth-moving equipment. Other chapters deal with ways to trash the head office of a corporation involved in projects offensive to environmental groups. Some of these, such as placing stink-bombs and jamming locks, are relatively innocuous. Dumping trash on the front lawns of those who dump it in the desert is also relatively harmless. However, another method they suggest, tree-spiking, can result in severe injury when a chain saw runs into the spike. If the spiked log arrives at a lumber mill, the spike can shatter a saw blade, sending fragments through the work area.

The avowed purpose of tree spiking is not to kill or injure people, but to cause economic loss and erode the thin profit margin. The costs of hiring guards for construction and logging sites, as well as the expense of installing surveillance equipment, cuts into profits. Economic warfare works, and a recent example in Britain, where animal-rights activists have been especially active, shows how effective it can be. Harrods, the British department store, announced in April, 1990, that it would shut down its fur salon.

Anti-smoking activists have threatened product tampering against supermarkets, sending letters warning of cyanide-laced cigarettes placed on store shelves. In 1986, letters arrived at three TV stations and one newspaper in San Jose, California, citing two stores where the poisoned cigarettes had allegedly been planted. Because product tampering is real, and has caused deaths in the past, ignoring the threat was impossible, although investigation in this case disclosed no tampering.[2]

Commercial Aircraft

There doesn't have to be any physical destruction to cause economic loss. A telephoned bomb threat can delay an airliner's departure, because the authorities can't ignore the threat, despite the resulting economic ripples. If the airliner's already left, the pilot will probably make an emergency landing at the nearest airport, passengers will arrive late, and some will even miss connecting flights. Airlines are willing to incur extra expenses to accommodate passengers in such situations, providing hotel rooms, meals, and even extra flights.

Bluff

Some terrorists use bluff because it often works, with widespread effects. The simplest form of bluff is to send a false fire alarm. This malicious prank ties up fire crews, keeping them unable to respond to genuine calls until they "clear" the false alarm. It also leads to traffic accidents involving responding fire engines.

In older cities with fire alarm boxes on every block, a false alarm prankster can simply pull the handle and run. Most cities today accept alarms by telephone, and some pranksters have used this method to call in many alarms. The ease of call tracing makes it mandatory to use public phones, because there are too many such telephones to guard them all. One New York City prankster appeared to be deadly serious, suspected of thousands of false alarm calls from public phones and his home in 1994. New York City's antiquated "911" system cannot trace calls.[3]

A canny saboteur can cause disruption without performing any overt act. A simple bomb threat is like turning in a false fire alarm. It can easily lead to the evacuation of a school or factory, stopping work until the threat is proved false.

"Coat-tailing" is a variation on this theme. When a real bomb explodes, it's usually followed by a rash of false alarms, and the authorities can't ignore them because they've just had proof that any threat might be real.[4]

A real-life bomber sometimes sends bomb threats as well, to taunt authorities and cause further disruption. When the Unabomber sent a letter to a San Francisco newspaper threatening to blow up an airliner out of Los Angeles International Airport in 1995, this caused a panic throughout California. Passengers were subjected to extra searches, even though the Unabomber is not a suicide bomber and has not blown himself up with his bombs. All mail was grounded, and passengers had to show photo I.D. at ticket counters. The enhanced security measures caused delays until the Unabomber sent a second letter admitting that it had been a prank.[5]

Food contamination is such a frightening prospect that a terrorist can force the recall of products with just a telephone call. In Tucson, Arizona, an anonymous caller to a TV station in 1990 stated that he had laced Thanksgiving turkeys at Smith's Supermarkets with cyanide. He refused to say how many turkeys he'd contaminated or how many stores were involved. Smith's immediately pulled all turkeys from its shelves, and offered refunds to customers who had already bought their turkeys at Smith's. Customers returned thousands of turkeys in response to the food chain's announcement.[6]

The prospect of liability ensures that practically all threats will have serious impact. If a terrorist "coat-tails" a threat of product tampering after a real one, a supermarket chain cannot ignore him. If the chain took no action, and death or injury resulted, even a mediocre ambulance-chasing liability lawyer would have an open-and-shut case of negligence.

Disruption Works

A society as complex as ours, with interdependent components and systems, suffers from the interruption of almost any part of its systems. A technically knowledgeable saboteur can cause great disruption and economic loss, without the customary blood-and-thunder terrorism. Some of the most intricate and sophisticated systems we have — computers — are especially vulnerable to subtle forms of sabotage, and we'll study these next.

Notes:

1. "Savvy Snipers Could Black Out Cities With Ease, Researchers Tell Congress," Associated Press, June 29, 1990.
2. "Stores' Cigarettes Poisoned, Letter Writer Claims," Associated Press, June 12, 1986.
3. Mokrzycki, Mike, "False Alarms: Man Suspected of Calling in Thousands of False Fire Alarms," Associated Press, December 9, 1994.
4. *Disruptive Terrorism*, Santoro, Victor, Port Townsend, WA, Loompanics Unlimited, 1984, pp. 100-101.
5. Lambropoulos, Dino, "Unabomber Says Threat A 'Prank,'" Associated Press, June 29, 1995.
6. "Supermarket Pulls Turkeys in Cyanide Poisoning Scare," Associated Press, November 23, 1990.

Chapter Eleven
Computer Sabotage

With the increasing importance of computers to business and government, computer sabotage has been increasing. During the 1970s, computer sabotage took the form of physical destruction. Today, high-tech methods such as "worms" and "viruses" allow the terrorist to damage data stored in computers without physical contact.

Fifty million computers are now potentially vulnerable to high-tech sabotage, partly because of the way people use them. There's widespread exchange of discs between computer users, and many employ "modems" to tap into central computers via the telephone lines. Computer networks and bulletin boards offer ready-made avenues for spreading destructive programs. This makes it unnecessary to break into a computer facility to destroy data.

Computer Crime and the Law

It's easy to pass a law, but another matter to enforce it. Several states have enacted legislation covering computer crimes of various sorts, following Arizona's Seminal computer crime law in 1980. Several police agencies now have special details of computer cops to investigate such crimes. But computer criminals and terrorists are typically more technologically sophisticated than the law enforcement and security officers investigating their actions, and they know how to evade detection. This is why so few get caught.

Practical Computer Sabotage

There are three approaches to sabotaging computers:
1. Physical destruction by explosion, fire, or mechanical means such as hammers and axes.
2. Damaging records, such as destroying floppy discs, hard drives, tapes and manuals.
3. Tampering with software. This includes purloining information, and insertion of worms and viruses. [1]

Destruction or damage of hardware requires very little in equipment, because computers, with all their high-precision parts, are very delicate. Hammers and pry bars provide access to their innards, but even pouring water onto a computer can cause damage by short-circuiting the boards and wiring. Cathode ray tubes, used in monitors, are very vulnerable to cracking with a hammer.

Destroying discs and tapes is mainly of nuisance value, because businesses routinely make duplicates.[2]

Physical destruction is crude, and usually requires the terrorist to make an appearance. New techniques allow destroying computer records and sabotaging computers, without requiring physical proximity in space or time. Various remote electronic techniques allow sabotaging computers from a distance. Others allow delayed-action effects, so that the terrorist is long gone when the destruction takes place.

Electronic Sabotage

Several high-tech methods have been developed, such as "worms" and "viruses," which allow the damaging of data stored in computers without entering the premises, and with minimal risk of apprehension. These make it very easy for the electronic terrorist.

A "worm" is a program, hidden inside an innocuous one, that will damage the data inside the host computer. One type of worm is the "logic bomb," a program that initiates destruction if a certain condition is met, or upon receipt of a certain signal or command. A simple and obvious method of electronic reprisal is to insert a hidden command to damage data if the originator's name is deleted from the payroll file. This provides a reprisal in case the company fires or lays off the originator. In September, 1988, Donald Gene Burleson was convicted of sabotaging a computer in a Fort Worth, Texas, insurance and brokerage company where he'd worked. Burleson had planted a logic bomb in the computer, eliminating 168,000 payroll records, as reprisal for his dismissal.

Burleson was not very subtle about it, which is why authorities apprehended him. He did not plant the program before his dismissal, but afterwards, and other employees reported seeing him inside the plant at a computer console.[3]

A worm which destroys a great deal of data at one blow, or locks up the computer system and prevents its use, is obvious, and the victim knows that something has suddenly gone terribly wrong. A simple form is the program with the DOS code "Del *.*" between two other lines. If properly formatted, this will erase everything on the active drive. A slightly more sophisticated version contains a line stating, "Del C:\ *.*" This will erase the hard drive.

Perhaps more destructive, and certainly more cruel, is the "data diddler" program, which introduces small errors into data, progressively and over a period of time. A simple example is the rogue command which reduces each customer's bill by a small percentage. This results in progressive monetary loss, and does not advertise its presence. Small errors are easily explicable as keyboarding errors, and may result in turnover of billing personnel before management discovers the real problem.

Another way of diddling data is to modify rate discs that insurance companies send to their agents periodically. This will result in a rash of misquotes, and a lot of time lost in correcting the errors. A more destructive way is to send a "Trojan horse."

A Trojan horse is the host program, which carries a worm or virus inside it. This allows entry as a seemingly innocuous program, and is a way of spreading a destructive program among computer users who exchange or regularly receive discs. Insurance agents who regularly receive discs from the home office, computer hobbyists who exchange discs, and customers of mail-order houses are vulnerable to Trojan horses. A Trojan horse is particularly pernicious when it contains a "virus."

Viruses

A "virus" is a type of sabotage program that replicates itself, so that several generations can infect other computers after the original target. These destructive programs are sometimes pranks, but can also serve malicious purposes.

A virus can be like cancer, replicating itself indefinitely. While some viruses are designed to make only one copy in a particular computer, drive or disc, other versions reproduce without stopping. These eventually take up all of the disc and memory, choking the computer. Although they're not destructive in the strictest sense, they effectively stop the computer from working.

The creator of a virus is an electronic firebug. His technical knowledge allows him to employ several methods to introduce his virus into other computers. One technique is by infecting a network, such as a computer bulletin board, directly. This will spread the virus to any computer that patches in. The virus design allows it to reproduce itself and transmit itself via modem, every time a customer goes "on-line."

Although the largest commercial bulletin boards claim to have safeguards against viruses, some electronic firebugs are very sophisticated. They know how to defeat electronic security measures. Some are employees or former employees of these firms, and can use their inside knowledge to bypass security measures. This gives them access to every computer that comes on-line. According to John McAfee, Chairman of the Computer Virus Industry Association, CompuServe, a major computer network service, was the victim of the "nVIR" during 1988.[4]

Not all viruses are terribly destructive. Some are actually humorous, such as the "Cookie Monster" virus. The virus flashes the message "I want a cookie" on the screen, locking up the computer's functions until the user types "cookie" on the keyboard. It can become annoying, however, to have work interrupted by the Cookie Monster.

There are about fifty million small computers in use by individuals and businesses. These are now vulnerable to high-tech sabotage, the method depending on how the owner uses his computer. Computer hobbyists who exchange discs can unwittingly spread viruses, progressively infecting others because the virus replicates itself in each system. Once such a disc plays on a system, the virus breaks out and infects the system. It will also write the virus program on any other disc passed through the system. Yet another way to spread a virus is to produce pirated versions of common applications programs, such as business and word processing programs, and even computer games.

Electronic AIDS

The most sophisticated virus creators have programmed incubation periods, which allow the virus to spread. This allows infecting many systems before anyone notices a malfunction that signals that a virus is on the loose. The longest incubation period encountered so far is about two years, but there is no technical reason why virus programmers can't produce longer periods. Because an incubating virus requires direct contact by disc or wire, and can take years to appear, meanwhile infecting other systems, it's the electronic equivalent of AIDS.

Electronic Bomb Threats

Even the threat of virus infection can cause computer down-time, while technicians search for the rogue program. A threat of virus infection is the electronic equivalent of a bomb scare. An anonymous telephone threat can cause the shutdown of a computer or computer network, because a security executive can't afford to ignore such a threat, especially if his employer's computer has already suffered virus damage.

A logic bomb can serve as a threat to obtain ransom. At times, this is outright criminal extortion. Another application is made by computer suppliers and programmers. They can install a program to incapacitate the unit, or destroy data, if the customer does not pay his bill on time.

Commercial Warfare

A computer virus is also useful for sabotaging a competitor's products. An unscrupulous software company executive could easily put infected versions of his rival's programs into the market, to alienate their clients. Another way is direct infection of computers at the factory. One 1990 outbreak resulted from a virus infection of the software discs packed with new modems. A major supplier, Compuadd, based in Austin, Texas, had obtained a supply of modems from GVC Technologies, Inc. These used programs duplicated by a Chinese company, and the duplication process was the apparent mode of entry.[5]

A 1995 survey by *Security Management* magazine revealed that 20 percent of the companies surveyed had suffered virus infections in their computers. One company reported having received an unsolicited promotional disc.[6]

A built-in weakness in many computer systems is called a "trapdoor." This is a quick way into the system, bypassing various levels of security, to allow servicing by technicians. In theory, service technicians are supposed to close or remove trapdoors after installation, but often they don't, or they leave one entry to make future servicing easier.[7]

Exploitation of trapdoors is what gives insiders an edge over those who have not been employees of a particular business. A person using a trapdoor for personal gain, or to plant a virus maliciously, may be an employee of the computer manufacturer, the software supplier, or the customer. When Robert Morris, Jr., did a number on the Arpanet system in 1988, he used a trapdoor to introduce his Internet WORM program.[8] This resulted in the infection of about 6,200 computers, a shutdown of an entire network, and a cleanup cost of over $98 million dollars.[9]

One innovative use of a trapdoor by a legitimate insider was when the computer software company Logisticon disabled software sold to Revlon after a dispute over a $180,000 bill in 1990. Logisticon executives decided that they were not going to let Revlon continue to use the software that Revlon hadn't paid for. Logisticon programmers used a modem to gain access to the software in Revlon's computer and put it out of action. In effect, this was electronic repossession.[10]

Countermeasures

The emergence of worms, viruses and other threats to computers has resulted in an entire new industry, overlapping with computer security specialists. Formerly, computer security people were concerned about data theft and physical sabotage, but today the threats are more far-reaching and comprehensive.

There are computer virus specialists, such as John McAfee, Chairman of the Computer Virus Industry Association, 4423 Cheeney Street, Santa Clara, CA 95054. People such as McAfee devise programs to counter viruses, and the names of some of these programs are both revealing and funny. One anti-virus program is called "VACCINATE," and it allegedly performs an electronic vaccination. Another, similar program is called

"IMMUNIZE." Yet another is the "DISK DEFENDER," and another is called "CONDOM."[11]

The latest versions of disc operating systems, such as IBM's PC-DOS 6.0 and 7.0, have built-in virus checkers. Utility sets, such as Norton, also have similar features. The user can check his drives manually, or program the system to run a check each time he turns on the computer, or at intervals.

Without special programs, protection against virus infection is still possible. There is no absolute protection, but it's practical to take steps to greatly reduce the risk from viruses and other threats.

A basic step is to create a back-up copy of all important data. A computer with a hard drive has copies of the applications programs on the drive, and the originals should be safely locked away. It's also necessary to back up all important data, in duplicate. This allows salvaging the data if a virus attack occurs.

Another precaution is to avoid accepting discs from new sources. Exchanging discs is very much like having sex in a public bathhouse in San Francisco. So is installing a modem and logging on to computer bulletin boards. Although the operators of most bulletin boards act in good faith, they may unwittingly become infection points.

There is a safe way of operating a modem, and an unsafe way, in the same sense that there is "safe sex" and "unsafe sex." "Safe" is not absolutely safe, but it avoids the greatest risks. Most modems have two settings, outgoing only, and incoming/outgoing. Setting a modem to accept incoming calls allows someone else to reach your computer and introduce any program he wishes, including a virus. Leaving the toggle switch on "outgoing" only prevents this. It doesn't prevent your downloading an infected program from a bulletin board or other source, however.

If you must use a modem, log on only to major commercial bulletin boards. They have a vested interest in protecting their subscribers, and more technical competence than small BBSs.

There are many anti-virus programs available, but the best of these are good only for checking a computer's memories to see if they've been infected. Most cannot detect all forms of worms or viruses, mainly because new ones are constantly coming to the fore.

Some symptoms of virus infection are: increase in processing time, inexplicable disappearance or alteration of data, and keyboard lockout. These are not sure signs of virus infection, but merely ambiguous symptoms which may have other causes. It's possible, for example, to erase a block of data inadvertently by striking the wrong key or combination of keys.

This points up the importance of duplication, or back-up. Backing up is protection against data loss from any cause, including total destruction of the computer.

With all data and programs on discs, the remedy for an infected computer is wiping its hard drive and all working discs. This usually involves reformatting everything, as this is the only way to ensure that no virus residue can remain dormant, ready to spring to life after the programs are once more installed. An "erase" command is not adequate, because this doesn't actually wipe out any memory.

Viruses are not as great a threat as some sensationalizers claim, but they are serious. The comparison with AIDS is apt. Like AIDS, the virus cannot spread through casual contact, such as being in the same room with an "infected" computer or disc. There has to be an electronic connection, analogous to blood contact with AIDS. Unlike AIDS, there is a sure cure for any computer virus infection. With sensible precautions, it's possible to avoid or cure the problem.

Notes:

1. *Ecodefense: A Field Guide to Monkeywrenching*, Second Edition, Foreman, Dave, and Haywood, Bill, Tucson, AZ, Ned Ludd Books, 1987, p. 213.
2. *Ibid.*, p. 216.
3. *Computer Viruses, Worms, Data Diddlers, Killer Programs, and Other Threats to Your System*, John McAfee and Colin Haynes, NY, St. Martin's Press, 1989, pp. 35-36.
4. *Ibid.*, p. 165.
5. Associated Press, October 6, 1990.
6. "Tales of Woe," *Security Management*, Volume 39, Number 5, May, 1995, p. 10.
7. *Computer Viruses*, pp. 77-79.
8. *V.I.R.U.S. PROTECTION (Vital Information Resources Under Siege)*, Pamela Kane, NY, Bantam Books, 1989, p. 6. Note: This book comes with a virus checking disc as part of the package.
9. *Computer Viruses*, pp. 5-7. This figure is in dispute, however. Pamela Kane, on p. 96 of her book, gives her reasons why she feels the actual cost was much less.
10. "No Payment, No Lipstick," *Time*, November 5, 1990, p. 57.
11. *V.I.R.U.S. PROTECTION*, p. 20.

Chapter Twelve
Kidnapping

In the United States, during the 20th century, kidnapping began as a for-profit enterprise by gangsters. It tends to be political elsewhere in the world, although Italian and Latin American criminal gangs also kidnap for ransom. Sometimes the two motives blend, as when a terrorist group kidnaps wealthy people to exchange them for money to finance their efforts.

Why are Americans often the victims of kidnapping overseas? Probably because we have more enemies, although a pragmatic view is that it is because we have more money than citizens of many other countries. Russians are rarely kidnapped outside of their native land, although the reason for this isn't clear. One story making the rounds is that Middle Eastern terrorists once kidnapped a Soviet official, and the Soviet response was to send a squad of KGB operatives who kidnapped a leader of the terrorist group. They returned him to the kidnappers in little pieces. The problem with this story is that, although widely repeated, it's never attributed to any specific individuals, and never states exactly where and when this incident took place.

Domestic political kidnapping isn't common, but incidents do occur. The Symbionese Liberation Army kidnapped Patty Hearst, daughter of the newspaper tycoon, during the early 1970s. The details regarding how the group treated her during captivity are murky, but the surprising result was that she became a convert to their cause, and took part in a bank robbery.

Tactics

There is a "tradecraft" to kidnapping, a protocol which is also useful when the purpose is assassination. Both professional and amateur attackers use these techniques, but with varying degrees of proficiency.

Reconnaissance

This is the first, and most important step in planning an attack. The attacker scrutinizes and evaluates his target before deciding how and when to attack. The attacker will shadow his target to find the moment and place when and where the target is most vulnerable and least protected. He'll also evaluate the situation with an eye towards the escape route, which is essential for the kidnapper, but not vital for the assassin who doesn't plan to escape or who is intent on losing his life during the act.

The victim's daily routine and personal weaknesses offer many opportunities for an attack. A target that appears at a certain place at the same time each day is merely setting himself up for an attack. A target who "ditches" his body-guards to keep an appointment for a sexual liaison also makes himself vulnerable if an attacker learns of this proclivity.

Planning

Kidnappers often capture their targets in transit, while they're away from the security of home or office. Once the kidnappers have a clear picture of their target's routine, they select the spot. In many cases, the attempt takes place within a block or two of home or office, mainly because it's very predictable that the target will be in the vicinity.

A noted kidnapping for extortion was that of Exxon International president Sidney Reso, snatched at the entrance to his own driveway at home in 1994. The kidnapper was a former security officer for Exxon, and therefore had an inside track on his target. [1]

Execution

Carrying out the plan is the last step, and if the kidnappers have carried out the first two steps competently, the act itself usually goes smoothly. In this regard, it doesn't seem to matter how many bodyguards encircle the victim. The kidnapping typically goes off well despite them.

Ransom

Kidnappers usually demand money or political ransom, which is often the release of some of their colleagues, whom they call "political prisoners." The negotiation for ransom is often tricky, either because the governments involved don't want to be seen as giving in to kidnappers, or because the negotiator is a game-player eager to display his psychological skills.

Sometimes, the victim suffers injury during the kidnapping, or his health fails during captivity. The result is a dead victim, or damaged goods. At that point, the kidnapping and ransom efforts fall apart, and the kidnappers have to flee or go underground to escape capture.

Kidnapping is not a growth industry right now. With sophisticated bugs that authorities can put into bundles of ransom money, and enhanced ways to trace currency, the prospect of a successful payoff has diminished. On the other hand, assassination is doing well.

Notes:

1. "Four Days in Hell," *Time*, September 15, 1992, p. 15.

Chapter Thirteen
Assassination

Assassination is an age-old terrorist technique that has fared well in this country. It's important to note that assassinations have a long history in the country. President Andrew Jackson was attacked by a gunman, both of whose pistols misfired. Several American presidents have been murdered, including Lincoln, Garfield, McKinley and Kennedy. Lesser public and semi-public figures assassinated in this country were Chicago Mayor Anton Cermak, Dr. Martin Luther King, Jr., John Lennon, Robert F. Kennedy, and Meir Kahane, himself a terrorist leader.

The streets can be very unsafe, because the assassin's target is away from the safety of his home. An ambush can take only seconds, and the result is riddled metal. (Photo by Tony Lesce.)

Assassination can be very final. As a spokesman for the Irish Republican Army stated after a bomb blast that had narrowly missed British Prime Minister Margaret Thatcher in 1984: "We only have to be lucky once. You have to be lucky always."[1]

Some political figures have survived multiple attempts. Charles de Gaulle survived 31 attempts. President Gerald Ford survived at least two. There were at least half a dozen attempts against Adolf Hitler.

Exporting Murder

Political assassination is more common in other countries, such as those in Latin America and the Middle East. However, some of these countries' terrorists have been exporting their violence to the United States. Orlando Letelier, former foreign minister of Chile, was blown up in his car in Washington, DC, in September, 1976, by killers sent from home to do him in. More recently, the Israeli Military Attaché, Colonel Yosef Alon, was shot to death by Middle Eastern terrorists outside his home in Chevy Chase, Maryland, on July 1, 1981.

On May 4, 1982, Orhan R. Gunduz, Honorary Turkish Consul to the New England States, was shot to death in Somerville, Massachusetts. An Armenian group took credit for the shooting. The Armenians took their campaign across the border as well. On August 27 of that year they shot Turkish Colonel Attilla Atikat, Military Attaché to Canada, to death in his car.

The Middle Eastern conflict has spread to American soil. A bomb exploded in the Orange County offices of the Arab-American Anti-Discrimination Committee in 1985, killing Alex Odeh. Meir Kahane, Jewish/Israeli militant and a terrorist himself, was shot to death by an Arab in New York City in 1990. After his death, members of Kahane's organization,

"Kach," sent death threats to several Americans they considered inimical to their cause.[2]

A collateral effect of the Middle Eastern situation was the bombing of a van driven by Sharon Rogers, wife of Will Rogers III, captain of the American cruiser U.S.S. Vincennes. On July 3, 1988, Captain Rogers' ship fired a missile that destroyed an Iranian airliner and killed its 290 passengers, including children. This mistake was hard to explain, because it took place in daylight, and an airliner doesn't look at all like a jet fighter.

Results came quickly. A few days after the destruction of the Iranian Airbus, Mrs. Rogers received a phone call from an unidentified person with an accent asking, "Are you the wife of the murderer?" In March, 1989, a bomb exploded under Mrs. Rogers' van as she was driving to work in San Diego. She was unharmed, but the van was gutted by fire and metal fragments.[3]

Civil-Rights Cases

The United States' inability to cope with minority problems exploded during the 1960s. On one side, there were widespread riots, and on the other various forms of killings of civil-rights activists. Medgar Evers, a civil-rights demonstrator, was shot to death from ambush on June 1, 1963, in Jackson, Mississippi. In 1966, at least two other civil-rights marchers, Viola Liuzzo and Jonathan M. Daniels, were assassinated in Alabama. On June 22, 1967, an unsuccessful assassination attempt against civil-rights leader Roy Wilkins took place in New York City.

Dr. Martin Luther King, Jr. was shot to death by an assassin's .30-06 bullet in the neck on March 4, 1968, and this shooting precipitated a series of ghetto riots in many major cities.

Killings continued after that. On May 29, 1980, a gunman shot Vernon Jordan, Urban League president, in Fort Wayne, Indiana. Jordan survived the assault.

On the other side of the racial line, Black Muslims shot and killed Malcolm X, who had recently defected from their cause, in 1965. Ironically, Malcolm X was killed on the first day of National Brotherhood Week. Fortunately, his killers were not white, as race riots might well have ensued if they had been, as they did after Dr. Martin Luther King, Jr.'s shooting three years later. However, a Black Muslim mosque in Harlem was torched, allegedly by some of Malcolm's followers, a few days later.

The Symbionese Liberation Army, another radical group, shot Marcus Foster, African-American superintendent of schools, in Oakland, California, in 1973. The reason for his murder was unclear.[4]

Abortion

Some of the most recent assassinations have been directed against abortionists and their associates. One Florida abortion doctor with the name of "Gunn" ironicically died by the gun, taking three bullets in the back in 1993. Abortionist Dr. George Tiller was shot in both arms while driving away from his abortion clinic in Wichita, Kansas, on August 19, 1993. Another Florida abortionist, Dr. John B. Britton, and his bodyguard/escort James Barrett, were shot to death in July, 1994.

Shootings of abortionists have spread north of the border. A Vancouver, British Columbia, physician who performs abortions took a bullet in his leg while at home one morning in 1994. A sniper fired three shots at the doctor, who was seated at his breakfast table. Dr. Garson Romalis survived the shooting.[5]

There emerged the prospect of more serious attacks. One man had planned to kill as many abortion supporters as he could in Florida, then commit suicide. Government agents arrested him and confiscated two handguns, one rifle, and 400 cartridges.[6]

An anti-abortion activist shot up two abortion clinics with fatal results in Massachusetts in December, 1994. A witness who described the scene made the understatement of the year: "He was very angry." [7] The next day, the suspect shot up the Hillcrest Clinic in Norfolk, Virginia, but nobody was hurt.[8]

Right-Wing Assassinations

Alan Berg was a talk show host operating on radio station KOA in Denver. He was one of those hosts who are known today as "shock jocks," specializing in bad taste and interviews designed to antagonize as many people as possible to boost his ratings. Berg began his career as a Chicago lawyer, but dropped out after his *petit mal* seizures interfered with his trade. He got into radio in the Denver area in 1975, and soon developed his provocative and vicious style, which involved mockery, name-calling, and hanging up on callers. Berg became known as "the man you love to hate," and reveled in playing up his Jewish origins and pro-Israeli sympathies, insulting Christians and right-wingers. To his misfortune, some of his listeners turned out to be both thin-skinned and homicidal.

The morning of his death in 1984, Berg began his radio talk show in typical style, insulting Roman Catholics. He may not have realized during his diatribes that his having a listed telephone made it easy for enemies to find his address. When he got home that evening, Bruce Pierce, member of the Silent Brotherhood, riddled him with .45 caliber submachine gun bullets as soon as Berg emerged from his shabby Volkswagen Beetle.[9]

Workplace Assassinations

During recent years there have been several widely-publicized killings by employees or former employees of businesses. These are not, strictly speaking, "terrorist" assassinations because the perpetrators were individuals. Nevertheless, they caused terror both in immediate multiple casualties and in long-range effects. Businesses are focusing more on workplace security and applicant screening today because of workplace violence.

In Asheville, North Carolina, a man who had been fired two days before for fighting with fellow employees returned to spray the workplace with gunfire. Using a .30-caliber carbine and a .38 Special revolver, he killed three and wounded two on May 17, 1995. His main targets appeared to be management. It was a sign of the times that, before his deadly reappearance, some employees expressed "black humor about him coming back and doing something," according to one employee. [10]

Post Office Killings

Given the persistent deterioration of service by the U.S. Postal Service, it's surprising that post offices aren't besieged by angry customers, but the fact is that post office shootings have all been by employees and ex-employees. Some people not employed by the post office have been caught in the crossfire. Patrick Sherrill killed 14 people in the Enid, Oklahoma, post office in 1986. In 1989, John Taylor killed his wife at home, then killed two postal employees and injured another at the post office before committing suicide. Joseph Harris shot his former postal supervisor and her boyfriend at home in October, 1991. He then went to the Ridgewood, New Jersey, post office to kill another two postal employees before giving himself up to police. In November of the same year, ex-postal employee Thomas McIlvane shot four supervisors and injured five other workers in Royal Oak, Michigan, then committed suicide. Mark Hilburn, another fired postal employee, shot two post office employees in Dana Point, California, on May 6, 1993. Three days later, Larry Jason killed one employee and injured two others before committing suicide at the Dearborn, Michigan, post office.

Miscellaneous Murders

Even those who do not occupy public office, work for the Postal Service, or involve themselves on one side or the other of the abortion controversy, are potential targets. Mark David Chapman, a security guard from Hawaii, stalked and shot to death John Lennon in New York City in December, 1980. The singer and his wife were walking into their apartment building at 10:30 P. M. when Chapman drew his Charter Arms .38 Special revolver and emptied five rounds into Lennon's back.[11]

An oddball killing was that of George Lincoln Rockwell, leader of the racist American Nazi Party, during the sixties. He was shot to death with a Luger pistol by one of his fellow members while coming out of a laundromat in Alexandria, Virginia.

Arthur Bremer, the smiling gunman, staked his claim to fame when he shot and paralyzed Southern politician George Wallace, who was then running for president, in Wheaton, Maryland, on May 15, 1972. Several shots from a short-barrel revolver took effect, one lodging in Wallace's spinal cord. This was not a murder, because Wallace survived, although paralyzed.

Assassination is not only an age-old tradition: It's here to stay. We can expect more political and workplace killings in the future, as tensions mount and desperate people break apart under pressure.

Notes:

1. Kelly, James, "We Have Only to be Lucky Once," *Time*, January 7, 1985.
2. Cockburn, Alexander, "The Kach Hit List," *The Nation*, v251, n23, December 31, 1990, p. 830.
3. "Bombs Across The Ocean?" *Time*, March 20, 1989, p. 26.
4. *Time*, February 18, 1974.
5. Associated Press, November 8, 1994.
6. Associated Press, March 16, 1994.
7. Trott, Robert W., "Clinic Shooting: Two Dead, Five Wounded in Shooting at Two Abortion Clinics," Associated Press, December 30, 1994.
8. Taylor, Joe, "Clinic Shooting: Clinic Shot up by Gunman Has History of Protests, Violence," Associated Press, January 1, 1995.
9. *The Silent Brotherhood*, Flynn, Kevin, and Gerhardt, Gary, NY, The Free Press, 1989, pp. 171-207.
10. Associated Press, May 18, 1995.
11. Jones, Jack "John Lennon's Killer; A Small Voice Said 'Do it! Do it! Do it!'; Decade Later, Killer Prays to be Forgiven," *USA Today*, December 3, 1990, p. 1A.

Chapter Fourteen
Law Enforcement Reactions

Our society depends on law enforcement for defense against crime, including terrorism. In fact, law enforcement is not as effective as some think it is, and the glamorized and idealized picture presented by TV "cop shows" is unrealistic.

The TV depiction of clean-cut, square-jawed, untiring investigators who always get their man is pure fantasy. Reality is far different and more prosaic. In real-life cases, most law enforcement preparation is simply a slight beefing up of security and waiting for the first blow to fall, then pursuing the perpetrators.

At the outset of the 1990-91 Persian Gulf crisis, the FBI was expecting a terrorist offensive by Saddam Hussein's sympathizers, and was on alert to forestall these anticipated attacks. Special measures included pumping the FBI's informers among Arabs living in America, enhancing electronic surveillance of Arabic-speaking people and groups, and reinforcing security at government office buildings.[1]

Another precaution was photographing and fingerprinting everyone entering the country using Iraqi or Kuwaiti passports. When the Iraqis invaded Kuwait, they also captured the office that issues travel documents.[2]

Other measures included setting up informer "hot lines," bringing potential target lists up to date, reviewing the preparedness of S.W.A.T. teams, instituting extra checking of I.D. cards, stopping and searching all vehicles at facility entrances, and being more ready to evacuate in response to bomb threats.[3]

Deportation of Aliens

The federal government has an array of plans for dealing with emergencies. One calls for the detention and subsequent deportation of aliens who pose a threat to national security.

National Security Decision Directive 207, issued by the president, and titled "The National Program for Combating Terrorism," calls for expulsion of "alien activists not in conformity with their immigration status." This broadly worded phrase includes not only terrorists, but aliens who are politically active, and those who are in technical violation, such as overstaying visas, holding jobs illegally, and not fulfilling student requirements.[4]

Restricting Immigration

At first glance, this seems a neat and practical way to reduce the influx of terrorists and of people who have trouble adapting to the American culture and who become social problems by their very existence. Regretfully, this doesn't seem to be a practical policy.

American borders are very porous, as evidenced by the millions who enter across the frontier with Mexico every year. We've been unable to stop the flow of illegal immigrants and illegal drugs for decades. Various proposals for constructing "Great Walls of China" to cope with this problem have proved to be too expensive or are in conflict with our Constitution.

Truly controlling legal and illegal immigration would require air-tight border controls and a very secure system of national identity cards. To enforce tightened immigration laws within the country would require regular identity checks, with police checkpoints at every airport, train and bus station, plus random checkpoints on the streets. Like the Chinese policy of only one child per family, this would be unworkable in America.

Rewarding Informers

In 1990, the U. S. government began publicizing its offer of reward money for tips about terrorists. Airlines banded together to collect another million dollars to supplement official funds in cases involving attacks on U.S. civil aviation.[5]

There have been several instances of people collecting reward money after furnishing the government information on terrorism. An important aspect of this policy is that the U.S. government will pay for information that averts a terrorist strike. The government is keeping quiet about exactly who claimed rewards for what information they've provided, but there has been some success so far for the $2 million paid out through 1995. The best success was a 1992 tip regarding a planned attack against the Bangkok facility of an American airline. [6] All told, it's a pretty safe allocation of funds because pay-offs are entirely dependent on the value of the information.

When the Alfred P. Murrah Federal Building in Oklahoma City was devastated by a truck bomb in 1995, the FBI immediately got into the picture because this was a crime against federal employees and federal property. The Department of Justice appealed to the public for tips, and within 24 hours had earmarked $2 million reward money for information leading to the apprehension of the perpetrators, sure signs that solid clues were lacking.

Unfortunately, the FBI's record for solving this type of crime is spotty at best. One of the alleged bombers, "John Doe #1," was apprehended a couple of hours after the blast by an Oklahoma State Trooper, not the FBI, on unrelated traffic and firearms charges. The other John Doe was later identified as someone unconnected with the crime, and the case is still unfolding at time of this writing.

The "Unabomber," who has been sending bombs through the mail for nearly two decades, is still at large, taunting the

FBI for its inability to identify him. This case shows the extreme difficulty of apprehending a terrorist.

Investigative Techniques

Normal criminal investigative techniques can also work against terrorists. It should be standard procedure to interview the families and friends of a suspected terrorist to elicit as much information as possible. A crucial point is compiling a list of all family members and associates, which is why the interviewer should milk sources for these names and their addresses. Other useful information is hobbies and interests, occupations, and preferences in cars, clothing, and entertainment.

Terrorists often live underground existences, staying away from family, friends, and their usual haunts. But terrorists are human too, and sometimes succumb to the temptation to seek out family members and friends. Staking out these possibilities can result in capture, or at least the opportunity to follow the terrorist back to other members of the group. Staking out doesn't necessarily mean placing a surveillance team to watch all of a suspect's family members and associates, which can be prohibitive in regards to investigative personnel. Telephone taps can be enough.

A telephone tap can produce good leads, even if the terrorist calls from a public phone, which is a normal security measure. The contents of conversations can provide information for follow-up, such as his present address, associates, and future plans. Obviously, it's unlikely that a terrorist will tell his mother that he plans to blow up a bank the following Tuesday, but if he arranges to meet her, police can stake out the meeting place.

With all that, law enforcement isn't always successful. The person who contaminated Tylenol in the Chicago area in 1982 was never caught. Whoever set eleven fires in Winter Haven, Florida, in 1991, remains at large.

At times, events show that the police can't even protect themselves. A group calling itself the "People's Liberation Army" conducted a terror campaign against California narcotics officers and caused several injuries. A bomb attached to a narcotics officer's car blew up and injured his stepson, who had found it. Another bomb, mailed to an officer's home in the 1980s, aroused the suspicion of his wife, who called the bomb squad. A package addressed to another officer's home contained poisoned chocolates. The campaign included taunting and threatening letters sent to three local law enforcement agencies and to a newspaper, describing the PLA's intention to bring the police force to its knees.

To police, the most frightening aspect of this terror campaign was that the PLA had found out where officers lived, and was striking them at home. Police officers, especially those assigned to narcotics, protect their home addresses for fear of reprisals by those they arrest, and the breaching of security posed an intolerable threat.

Wargaming

An unconventional method of planning to meet a crisis is to stage a "wargame." This is a scenario in which selected personnel represent all of the players, including law enforcement, civilian government, the media, and terrorists. All parties try to behave in the manner they feel the real-life people would in the situation. Often, one side or both finds that they've made serious mistakes in handling the situation, and this is safer than making the same errors when real terrorists strike. After the game ends, personnel conduct a critique. This reveals the thought processes behind the actions, and offers an opportunity to correct shortcomings.

Wargames can be very realistic, and even predictive. One wargame, held in July, 1979, staged the hijacking of TWA

Flight 847 from Athens by terrorists, and followed it to a resolution. This closely paralleled the actual hijacking of the real TWA Flight 847, which took place on June 14, 1985. During the scenario, players simulated negotiations, the killing of an Israeli and an American passenger, and liaisons with other countries with an interest in the affair. The game ended with the payment of $50 million to the terrorists by the United States, payment of $10 million by Israel, and Israel's releasing 20 prisoners, in exchange for release of all remaining hostages.[7]

Wargames offer opportunities to try out innovative strategies and tactics, which in real life might seem too risky at first. For example, in the above scenario the players were free to enter negotiations and even pay ransoms, which might be politically impossible during a real hijacking. Even more importantly, wargaming makes it possible to test various actions by one's allies, actions which the real-life allies might not consider trying. A wargame can provide a testing ground for innovative solutions, and the players can run the game as many times as necessary in various configurations.

Technological Means

Using advanced technology to prevent terrorism and detect perpetrators is a mixed bag. On one hand, we have charlatans promoting "psychological profiling" techniques of limited value. This psycho-babble can be an investigative help in certain cases where the suspect list is limited, but a "profile" that can fit half a million people in the country is not much practical help in an investigation. A profile also is definitely not evidence that will stand up in court.

The physical sciences offer much greater promise. Cutting edge techniques can bring out what was undetectable until a few years ago.

One excellent example is the cellular telephone interceptor. Many believe that a cell-phone provides immunity to tracing, but anyone who watched the slow-speed chase of O.J. Simpson on TV knows that this is not so. His call from a cell-phone was traced, and soon police were following the White Bronco on Los Angeles freeways.

A lightweight device which can be used to trace a caller's cell-phone number is the Cellphone ESN Reader. This stores and prints up to 99 numbers, with times and dates. This is available from:

> Curtis Electro Devices
> 4345 Pacific Street
> Rocklin, CA 95677
> Phone: (800) 332-2790
> Fax: (916) 632-0636

Another hand-held device is a cellular call interceptor that can target multiple numbers, lock on to a visible target, monitor both sides of a conversation, and scan for calls in progress. The CT100A is available from:

> Cellular Technology
> 360 Connecticut Avenue, #285
> Norwalk, CT 06854
> Phone: (800) 215-2261

Wiretapping is likely to enter a new era. One reason is the proliferation of electronic bulletin boards, some of which are maintained by right-wing groups. These serve as information exchanges for recipes for explosives, guerrilla tactics, etc. A few are repositories for hit lists, names of the group's enemies, and a guide for terrorists seeking targets.

Weapon detection is an important means of protecting public buildings. Metal detection gates are common these days at airports and in some public buildings such as courthouses. More discreet devices that can focus in on selected individuals without their being aware of the electronic "frisk" are in the works. A millimeter wave camera that detects blockage of the body's natural radiation by a large metallic object is one way police and security officers could spot weapons in a crowd of people. Other electronic devices under development may fill gaps in existing security.[8]

Legislation

Many people, especially legislators, believe that the way to solve a problem is to pass a new law. The problem with legislators is that their main product is passing new laws, whether they're needed or not. They pass new laws based on the tacit assumption that they plug a gap in existing legislation. This is usually not so.

Among those who think this way are educated and sophisticated people who should know better. A law is merely a scrap of paper, and a simple-minded effort to cope with a problem. Still, we see the same array of outraged editorials and demands for stricter laws after every incident. After every terrorist act, there's a call for more anti-gun or anti-terrorist legislation, heavier penalties, more police protection, and more security. This is merely "feel-good" legislation, not worth the paper on which it's printed.

One excellent example of a useless law proposed by someone who should know better is the one suggested by Southern Poverty Law Center founder Morris Dees to the Senate Judiciary Committee in 1995. Dees would like to see "a federal law that would curb paramilitary training that is not authorized by state law."[9] The futility of this proposal is obvious, because tens of millions of Americans have received first-class military training courtesy of the U.S. government. Paramilitary training conducted by private groups is far inferior to the training the military establishment provides, and hardly worth any concern. The various "militias" causing current concern are practically useless as military forces for this reason.

There's also a danger of legislation banning paramilitary manuals, books on explosives, etc. Ten years ago, this was a bad idea because of the many such books in circulation and because such a ban, even if ruled constitutional, would immediately create a black market. Today it's totally futile, because the information is so widespread. There are bomb-making recipes on the Internet, and any subscriber can download all the information he needs.

A negative feature of new laws, especially "anti-terrorist" laws, is that they provide a terrorist with special status. It's more effective to prosecute terrorists under existing laws because their constitutionality has already been established in the courts.[10]

Realistically, these are hysterical reactions, not well-thought-out countermeasures. Let's look at why:

New laws are not the answer, because the most they can provide is a rewording of existing laws. A criminal or political terrorist intent upon murder will laugh at gun control laws because he can obtain firearms on the black market.

Firearms laws are perhaps the worst example of anti-crime legislation, especially when enacted with terrorism in mind. The worst mass murders in American history, the 1990 fire-bombing of a Bronx key club, which killed 87 people, and the 1995 Oklahoma City bombing which resulted in at least 168 fatalities, did not involve firearms. No gun control law can prevent putting together a fuel oil and fertilizer bomb, or a gasoline fire-bomb. A seven-day waiting period on fertilizer purchases will not affect the terrorist who decides to use a gasoline bomb. Banning all explosive or combustible substances, even if it were possible, would have absolutely no effect on product tampering. Finally, terrorists can succeed in putting across a hoax, as with the 1984 Mars Bars incident.

New legislation is futile if existing laws are inadequately enforced, and this is almost always the case.

Police protection doesn't work very well, because the police are a reactive force which comes to take a report after the event. The job of the police, local or federal, is to investigate crimes and apprehend the perpetrators. However, some have suggested a more pro-active role for police.

Infiltration and Undercover Investigations

While there have been calls for the FBI to infiltrate and investigate more potentially violent groups, this proposed course of action offers little hope for several reasons.

One is constitutional. The FBI or any police force cannot be an effective proactive investigating agency without trampling on American citizens' constitutional rights. Using informers is wide-spread, and can lead easily to abuses. ("Informer" is the correct term for a snitch or paid undercover agent. The term "informant" is often incorrectly used in its place. An "informant" is a witness to a crime or other uninvolved person, whereas an "informer" is a person who betrays his co-conspirators to police in return for money or leniency on another charge.)

It's also a fact that informers and leads, which ostensibly provide early warning of terrorist attacks, are often false alarms. Informers will concoct "information" for venal reasons, and a tedious task for a police officer working an informer is separating the valid information from the garbage.

Michael Levine, former federal agent, stated that about 15,000 out-of-control informers are directing the courses of cases, according to a *National Law Journal* report. Law enforcement officers paid informers $25 million in 1985, and by 1993 this had increased to $97 million. Some informers earn in payments several times what law enforcement officers earn in salary. Emad Salem, the informer who testified against the Moslem fundamentalists who blew up the World Trade Center, earned more than $1 million, even though his information did not come in time to prevent the bombing.[11]

Another problem with informers is that their records are often none too clean, and this impairs their credibility in court.

The record of Emad Salem, witness in the World Trade Center bombing trial, inspired criticism by both defense and prosecution. He had also admitted lying both to American immigration officials and to the FBI.[12]

One of the surprising points brought out at the trial of the World Trade Center bombers was that the FBI had begun surveillance of the group in 1989, four years before the blast. The FBI placed wiretaps on the telephone of one of the defendants ten days before the bombing. Emad Salem, the million-dollar informer for the FBI, stated that he'd warned the FBI that "a major bombing was imminent." These developments raised disturbing questions regarding the FBI's failure to prevent the bombing.[13]

The lessons are clear. Informers and infiltrators are very inconsistent. Some are worse than useless because of their venality and mendacity. Others are simply "flaky." Some, however, can be very valuable because they develop strong loyalty to their control officers.

Another problem comes to light when employing informers. A professional terrorist group practices security and counter-intelligence. The group's security officer keeps tabs on members, and is alert for police penetrations and suborning of members. If the group becomes aware that one of its number is playing games with the authorities, it won't necessarily execute him. There may be an attempt to "play back" the informer, turning him into a triple agent. This can produce very misleading information for the police.[14]

The problem lies in evaluating each informer and in correct handling. This requires an experienced control officer who has good judgment and good "people skills." Most importantly, the control officer must not let ambition or the eagerness to make a case override his skepticism, as so often happens.[15]

Can the FBI Be Effective?

Another problem is historical. The FBI, although it has received very favorable publicity over the years, has had its failures. During World War II, it broke up a German sabotage ring which landed by submarine, only because one member of the ring got cold feet and defected to the FBI a few days after landing. Without this defector to make it aware of the ring, the FBI would not even have known of its presence until defense plants began exploding.

While occupied with the urgencies of World War II, the FBI did not prevent the extensive atomic espionage carried out by the Soviet espionage services. The Rosenberg spy ring was not apprehended until after the Soviet Union had detonated its first nuclear bomb. Even then, the FBI was unable to round up all of its members.

From the middle 1960s to the middle 1980s, members of the Walker spy ring were able to pilfer many of the U.S. Navy's cryptographic secrets for the Soviets without the FBI becoming aware of their activities. The FBI arrested John Walker and his cohorts in 1985 only after Walker had retired from the U.S. Navy, and then mainly because his estranged wife snitched him off to them. Even then, the first FBI agent to interview her did not take her seriously.

The "Unabomber" is still at liberty. His letter to *The New York Times* mocked the FBI's efforts. "It doesn't appear that the FBI is going to catch us any time soon," he wrote, and added, "The FBI is a joke."[16]

The FBI is not alone. Like its record of clearing lesser crimes, law enforcement's record against terrorists is spotty. New York's Mad Bomber had 16 years of freedom before a massive and prolonged police effort identified him. It's not wise to place too much confidence in police efforts.

Psychological Methods

During the last couple of decades, police officials have called in psychologists to help in apprehending terrorists, as well as other types of lawbreakers. Psychologists draw up protocols for hostage negotiations, and "talking down" would-be suicides. This has done some good, but there have also been failures.

A major problem is that a psychologist or psychiatrist who tries to diagnose someone without interviewing him is walking on a razor's edge. This borders on charlatanism, and sometimes has serious repercussions.

One example is the Unabomber, whom the FBI tried to taunt in the hope of forcing him to make a mistake that would lead to his capture. Instead, he's continued with his deadly attacks.

Disposal of Terrorists

Europeans have found that imprisoned terrorists may become focal points for other terrorist efforts. A typical demand from hostage-takers is the release of their "imprisoned brothers," making convicted terrorists serious liabilities. A tacit method of coping with the problem has taken hold among some anti-terrorist teams: "take no prisoners." In practice, this means that if there's any resistance, terrorists will not survive the experience. Hostage rescue operations often end with assault team members giving each terrorist, "Two in the chest and one in the head, that's the way to make sure the fucker is dead."

Shoot-outs on American soil have sometimes resulted in the demise of all persons in the encircled premises. The Symbionese Liberation Army siege of 1974 involved several thousand rounds of ammunition, and ended when police shot burning tear gas grenades inside the building. Burning type grenades are prone to start fires, and these did. The owner of the house survived the attack.

Another incident that ended in flames was the FBI siege of Robert Jay Matthews on Washington State's Whidbey Island in 1984. Agents were ordered to shoot M-79 Starburst flare grenades into the house to start a fire. Matthews died in the fire. After the siege ended, an FBI agent told the press that the fire "was not started intentionally." But realistically, knowing what they did of the incendiary properties of the magnesium flares, there's no doubt that this fire was not exactly a surprise to the FBI commander.[17] There's little doubt that a similar process took place at the siege of the Branch Davidian compound at Waco, Texas, in April, 1993, although the victims were not a terrorist group. A complex of wooden buildings went up in a spectacular pyre, and the result was that most adults and all of the children on the premises died.

Extra-Territorial Arrest

The United States has, in several instances, arrested and brought back to this country those accused of crimes against American citizens overseas, under Title 18, Sections 1203 and 2331. This is blatant kidnapping, but court decisions have held that these cases would not be thrown out of court. The U.S. Supreme Court supported this principle, even when cases involve people who are forcibly brought from foreign countries which have extradition treaties with the United States.

This policy works, but it must be applied with great discretion. Foreign countries may not like the idea of American agents spiriting people out of their territories for trial in the United States any better than Americans would like foreign police officers taking American citizens overseas for prosecution.

Reprisals

One solution advocated by some is carrying out reprisals against terrorists and/or the states that sponsor them. This has been the Israeli policy for decades, and many cite the Israeli example as a way to handle the problem. Benjamin Netanyahu, an Israeli Government official, openly advocates reprisal for the sake of "deterrence."[18] In fact, Israel still has the problem and is still under terrorist attack, despite vigorous and extensive reprisals.

The main objection to reprisals is that they strike mainly at innocent people who may become radicalized by the violent reaction. Bombing an Arab village kills innocent persons, and survivors who had been previously uninvolved will now have a reason for becoming involved: revenge. Reprisal as policy is also unworkable in the case of domestic terrorism. Shelling or bombing a portion of an American city because a terrorist or members of his family live or once lived there isn't the same as bombing Beirut or Tripoli.

Civilians died when President Reagan ordered an air strike against Libya in 1986 in reprisal for the bombing of a Berlin nightclub earlier that year in which American soldiers were killed. Worse, Khaddafi hasn't reformed, but has merely become more subtle in sponsoring terrorism against Americans. He had a hand in the bombing of the Pan Am 747 over Lockerbie.

There were several reprisal attacks against Saddam Hussein, one coming after an abortive plot to kill former President Bush during his visit to Kuwait in 1993. President Clinton ordered a cruise missile attack against Iraqi intelligence headquarters, but the Iraqis claimed that missiles also fell in residential areas, killing civilians.[19] The aftermath is that Saddam Hussein is still in power, with his people united against the external threat.

Playing at reprisals is a dangerous game. Striking directly at a terrorist in a surgical attack appears to avoid involving innocent persons, but such an attack can still go wrong. The Israeli hit team members who killed a Moroccan waiter in 1973 in Lillehammer, Norway, in the mistaken belief that he was Ali Hassan Salameh, the Black September leader, shot their country's policy in the foot. One result was a public outcry that resulted in the disbanding of the commando unit.[20]

Overall, reprisals are simply tit-for-tat terrorism. They tend to be indiscriminate, and recent history has shown that reprisals don't work well at all.

Use of Force

Unlike reprisals, using force in a pre-emptive or reactive manner is rational, if competently performed. At times, it's necessary to fight fire with fire. There are several legitimate applications of deadly force against terrorists. Police and military armed response teams can cope with critical incidents, such as airplane hijackings, hostage-takings, attacks against critical targets, and high-risk arrests. Many police departments have S.W.A.T. teams, although these are probably not a match for hardened and dedicated terrorists.

The military have special units, such as Delta and the Navy Seal teams, which have both the weapons and training for heavy-duty enforcement. One scenario that would justify the use of a military team is the use of a nuclear weapon. Only industrial-strength action could cope with this sort of situation.

Legitimate use of a special response team would have several objectives:

The first is to save lives. Terrorists posing imminent danger to innocent persons are fair game, and thwarting a terrorist group during an attack in progress would spare innocent lives. An armed response team also serves as protection for a dignitary, such as the president, who is likely to be attacked.

Another is to identify the terrorists, if immediate apprehension isn't possible. An example is a group demanding money and an aircraft while holding hostages. Humanitarian considerations could easily force the authorities to let the terrorists escape, but knowing who they were would allow tracking them down once the hostages were out of danger.

Preventing the escape of terrorists is another legitimate purpose, if humanitarian considerations don't override this. In some situations, such as the location and identification of a terrorist headquarters, an armed response team would first attempt to force surrender, but if this failed, would then employ whatever force was necessary to capture or kill the terrorists.

Yet another purpose for a special team is to secure and process a crime scene, because often the law enforcement response comes too late to prevent the attack. Interviewing survivors, securing physical evidence, and preparing for a prosecution are crucial if the case is to be handled according to our laws.

Use of force must be judicious in order not to backfire against the government. Both law and public opinion support use of force when it's in proportion to the threat. A take-no-prisoners attack against a terrorist group armed with a nuclear or chemical/biological weapon of mass destruction would appear to be legitimate. However, when a group poses no measurable threat to the community, such as the Branch Davidians at Waco, and can be isolated and contained while the situation is sorted out, there is no justification for a totally destructive action. The presence of innocent persons, such as children, compels even more caution.

Pre-emptive force means neutralizing terrorists by various means to keep them from carrying out future attacks. These are the province of the "dirty tricks department."

The Dirty Tricks Department

There is an array of covert actions which are useful against terrorists, but may not be justified against ordinary criminals. These tricks, such as use of force, can backfire against the user, which dictates that they must be used with good judgment and great care.

One fairly safe dirty trick is the reverse sting, in which a fake illegal arms dealer sells defective weapons to terrorists. One such effort led to overly-sensitive detonators being provided to terrorist bombers in the 1980s. The result was a premature detonation that killed some members.[21]

Providing terrorists with defective weapons and other equipment can cause casualties, but there are other benefits as well. Concealing a "bug" inside the equipment can provide police with a way of eavesdropping on conversations. Another type of transmitter works as an electronic locator, allowing police to track movements.

"Turning" a member of the group to inform on his colleagues is conventional police work. Promising immunity from prosecution is one way to elicit cooperation, just as a false promise of immunity is one way to bring out a confession.

It's difficult to obtain much useful information from informers if the terrorist movement is compartmentalized, and impossible if the person arrested is a freelancer. There are other choices, though, that can produce results.

Another proactive approach is to foment dissent and distrust among the members of a terrorist group. One way is to arrest a group member and let him go after a few hours. Soon afterward, police arrest another member of the group, and let it slip that the other informed on him to save himself. The second member will get the news out to the rest of his group, who will probably decide to eliminate the "informer." Several such incidents can demoralize a group, as they begin distrusting each other.

Police interrogators can play several scenarios in the mind game against terrorists. One set-up is to question an arrested member regarding the activities of another member of the group. During the interrogation, a senior officer enters, listens for a minute, and instructs the interrogator, "Don't bother with that. We know all about him already."

Planting evidence is one way of finding a pretext for an arrest and prosecution. There simply may not be any court-room evidence to permit prosecution of a terrorist, and a short-cut is to plant a quantity of illegal drugs in his residence or car. In jurisdictions with severe gun laws, planting a firearm or destructive device will do.

There are several ways of planting evidence. One is to recruit an informer within the group to do the planting. Another way is by surreptitious entry. At times, planting evidence is very simple. In hot climates, when motorists leave their windows open a crack when parking, it's easy to slip a "baggie" of drugs through the crack and onto the seat. Having contraband in plain sight provides probable cause for search and arrest, and it's not too difficult to arrange for a uniformed police officer to be on the scene to make the arrest.

The ultimate dirty trick is, of course, killing a dangerous terrorist before he can mount another attack. This falls under covert operations, and requires specially employed and trained personnel. Killing is justified if there's no other way, or if lesser measures are too uncertain.

The main principle in killing a terrorist by extralegal means is positive identification, because an error can backfire with severe consequences. In case of uncertainty, it's wiser to refrain from pulling the trigger than risk killing an innocent person.

The choice of means of demise can be crucial. Shooting is fairly safe, if the shooters know what they're doing and to whom. Explosives are indiscriminate. A boobytrap can kill or maim an innocent person, which is why great care is necessary to ensure that only the target is within the lethal radius of the bomb.

The dirty tricks department can be very useful, despite some moral reservations. It's unwise to allow conventional morality to inhibit the elimination of a dangerous terrorist who has already killed and is likely to kill again. It's important never to forget that saving lives is the main purpose of anti-terrorist covert action, and that a terrorist who is allowed to live out of misguided morality may kill again. The government official who spares the lethal terrorist bears part of the responsibility for his killing other innocent persons, and the terrorist's victims' survivors won't thank him.

Negotiate With Terrorists?

From time to time, a government official makes a firm statement that his government will not negotiate with terrorists. Presumably, terrorists are so contemptible that they're not worth notice. Some terrorists, in turn, encourage this sort of response by announcing their unwillingness to negotiate.

The "theory" behind this stance is that any negotiations with terrorists accord them status they do not deserve, and demean the government doing the negotiating. It's hard to justify such a posture. Police negotiators will talk with an ordinary criminal, and negotiation is a well-established technique.

Also, the attendant theory goes, negotiations and concessions offer incentives to other terrorists to try it again. Nobody makes this claim when the lawbreaker is an ordinary stickup artist or bank robber, which makes it difficult to justify refusing to negotiate with terrorists.

Refusing to negotiate with terrorists sounds like the moral high ground, but it's cheap posturing, the executive equivalent of feel-good legislation. It also doesn't work. Many countries have stated that they will not negotiate with terrorists, but this hasn't made the terrorists go away. Some, such as Israel, have taken this hard line, but when the crunch came they negotiated anyway, as in 1968 when Israel released political prisoners. Refusing to negotiate is unrealistic because this position abandons the tactical advantages of negotiation.

A softer line is politically and tactically practical, especially when innocent persons are hostages. This becomes crucial if children are involved, because political pressure may force a government executive to abandon his no-negotiation posture.

There are humanitarian reasons that may dictate a softer, conciliatory approach, to save lives. Negotiation can obtain the release of hostages, and terrorists can always be captured and punished later.

Most importantly, negotiation keeps open an important avenue of action. Negotiation is a time-proven and important technique, and helps the information-gathering effort.

We have only to look at Waco to see what can happen when a government official abandons negotiations. The official FBI position on Waco is to place all the blame for not surrendering on David Koresh, thereby ignoring the stupidity of government officials in ordering an assault in a situation that was well-contained and under control.

A compromise that sometimes takes place is "back-channel" negotiations, using an intermediary that the government can disown if negotiations don't progress to its liking. Officially, the government can simply say "no comment" during the incident, while conducting negotiations towards a peaceful solution.

The Israelis used back-channel negotiations through a retired Israeli army officer who spoke with Ugandan dictator Idi Amin by telephone, in the hope of unofficially obtaining the release of hostages at Entebbe in 1976. In fact, the hostage-takers did release many hostages after a few days of captivity. Only when the negotiations did not seem to be producing further results did the Israeli government decide to send its commandos on the high-risk rescue.

These are some benefits of opening negotiations:

The negotiator can obtain a clearer picture of the terrorists and their goals.

The negotiator can "size them up," gaining an impression of their determination and their reliability. At times, suspects also let information slip regarding their weapons, location, future plans, and other information that affects the tactical situation. This can be very useful in planning an assault or rescue operation.

A skilled negotiator can obtain release of some or all hostages, as a "good faith" gesture. This reduces the problems a tactical team will face if an assault becomes necessary. Released hostages can provide valuable information regarding the number of hostage-takers, their locations, weapons, and even plans. They can also provide information that allows negotiators to appraise the terrorists' personalities, and decide which approach is best.

Even when no hostages are directly involved, negotiation is tactically valuable because it provides the opportunity to play for time while planning an attack, and the opportunity to turn the situation around and obtain serious concessions from the terrorists.

The best course to take during a terrorist incident, or any crisis, is not to close off possible courses of action. Announcing that an issue is "non-negotiable," or that the principle involved is more important than human lives, can lead to an untenable position and later recriminations. Remaining inflexible is worse than doing nothing at all.

A Partial Solution

Law enforcement can't do it all, which is why terrorists proliferate. Private citizens, understandably lacking confidence in law enforcement's ability to protect them, have turned to private security for another layer of defense.

Notes:

1. Meddis, Sam, "FBI Very Alert For Terrorism," *USA Today*, September 27, 1990, p. 4A.
2. Lacayo, Richard, "Saddam's Secret Weapon," *Time*, January 21, 1991, p. 35.
3. Meddis, Sam, "Terrorism Threat Real, Lasting; Expect to See Tighter Security," *USA Today*, January 18, 1991, p. 9A.
4. Pell, Eve, "Secret I.N.S. Deportation Plan: Kicking Out Palestinians," *The Nation*, v250, n5, February 5, 1990, p. 167.
5. Sharn, Lori, "Airlines Set to Offer $1M for Terrorists," *USA Today*, April 2, 1990, p. 3A.
6. Castro, Janice, "The Terrorist Bounty Hunters," *Time*, August 10, 1992. Grapevine, p. 11.
7. *War Games*, Allen, Thomas B., NY, Berkley Books, 1987, pp. 258-266.
8. "Exposing Concealed Weapons," *Law Enforcement News*, Vol. XXI, No. 419, March 15, 1995, p. 1.
9. Hutchinson-Hunter, Darlene, "Monitoring Militias," *Police Marksman*, Vol. XX, No. 4, July/August, 1995, p. 44.
10. *Disruptive Terrorism*, Santoro, Victor, Port Townsend, WA, Loompanics Unlimited, 1984, p. 31.
11. "Informants: Law Journal Says Use of Snitches 'Out of Control.'" Associated Press, February 12, 1995.
12. Neumeister, Larry, "Terrorism Trial: Government's Main Witness Flawed, Everybody Admits," Associated Press, January 30, 1995. Neumeister, Larry, "Trade Center Bombing: Key Prosecution Witness Admits Lying," Associated Press, March 22, 1995.
13. Neumeister, Larry, "Trade Center Bombing: FBI on Trail Nearly Four Years Before Blast," Associated Press, February 2, 1995. Neumeister, Larry, "Terror Trial: FBI

Orchestrated Terror Case to Salvage Its Reputation," Associated Press, January 31, 1995.

14. *Disruptive Terrorism*, Santoro, Victor, Port Townsend, WA, Loompanics Unlimited, 1984, pp. 112-113.

15. An incident that took place while the author was working on an article about a local Bureau of Alcohol, Tobacco, and Firearms team illustrates one of the dangers of informers. One June morning in 1991, the Phoenix office's "Achilles" team raided an apartment in South Phoenix, serving a search warrant based on information gleaned from an informer. Allegedly the occupant, who was out on parole, was dealing in illegal drugs and possessed a firearm. Possessing a firearm is illegal for convicted felons, under federal law.

One husky team member knocked the door down with a battering ram, while the leader and the others charged in. They emerged almost immediately almost gagging at the odor inside. One team member commented that "There must be a dead body in there." Team members, holding their breaths, re-entered and turned on the air conditioner and opened windows. The apartment obviously had not been cooled for the last couple of days. One officer found the source of the horrible odor: chicken parts in a plastic bag in the garbage can. A search produced no illegal drugs and no guns. During the search, the occupant came trucking up the walk and asked what the team was doing. He admitted living in the apartment, denied selling drugs, and explained that he had spent the weekend at his mother's home a few blocks away.

The team leader looked extremely unhappy at the way events had developed. At this point, the author asked him quietly: "John, do you ever get the feeling that some snitches are working both sides of the street?" The team leader replied glumly: "Yeah."

16. Lemonick, Michael, "The Bomb is in The Mail," *Time*, vol. 145, no. 19, May 8, 1995, p. 70.
17. *The Silent Brotherhood*, Flynn, Kevin, and Gerhardt, Gary, NY, The Free Press, 1989, pp. 381-382.
18. *International Terrorism*, Kegley, Charles W., NY, St. Martin's Press, 1990, p. 187.
19. Collins, James, "Striking Back," *Time*, July 5, 1993, p. 20.
20. Livingstone, Neil C., "Proactive Responses to Terrorism," *International Terrorism*, Kegley, Charles W., Editor, NY, St. Martin's Press, 1990, p. 225.
21. *Ibid.*, p. 224.

Chapter Fifteen
The Role of Private Security

Some years ago, expenditures on private security began to exceed money spent on official police. There were several reasons for this. The first is that the police cannot be everywhere, nor can the police protect everybody. In fact, several court decisions have held that the police are under no obligation to protect a specific person from crime. The police function is reactive. Police officers arrive after a crime has taken place, take a report, and pursue an investigation which may or may not be successful.

Wealthy people and businesses with assets to protect cannot depend on public police to provide adequate protection. Private security is preventive, unlike the reactive official police. Also, unlike official police, private security agents have limited arrest powers, which dictates that they operate in a pro-active and protective manner. The prevailing viewpoint is that prevention is better than cure.

A Growth Industry

This is why expenditures for private security have grown from about $20 billion in 1980 to $64 billion in 1995. Expert projections are that by the end of the decade, the amount spent on private security will be about $103 billion. The security industry's employees add up to about three times the number of local, state, and federal law enforcement personnel. As bodyguards, private and corporate uniformed security guards, and other personnel, they're found in all areas of the country, and the demand is increasing.[1]

Upscale housing developments have relied on armed or unarmed private guards to control access to their premises. Coupled with walls and gates, private guards can provide on-the-spot and around-the-clock protection. The net effect is that residents live in luxurious prisons of their own making.

Even lower-economic housing now employs security guards, because of crime and drug-related incidents. In a few cases, these are off-duty city police officers, but hiring private civilian guards is cheaper. Today, many school districts employ security guards because of the increase in school violence.

Businesses with extensive security needs rely on private protection, usually using an in-house guard force directed by a security manager. Smaller businesses, and some shopping malls, rely upon "rent-a-cops" for security. Companies with high-technology projects or government contracts have specially secured areas for their high-security work. The Department of Defense requires contractors to observe written guidelines for security, as a counter-measure against espionage or sabotage.

Private security is a growth industry. Even public agencies rely upon private security for some of their needs. For example, security personnel manning the gates and X-ray machines at airports are usually not police officers. Instead, they are rented from private security agencies for this low-grade work, and backed up with a small force of real police officers. The reason is that cost-conscious airport administrators feel that low-paid private security guards can perform these low-grade tasks as efficiently as more costly police officers. A few police officers are assigned as backups, in case a violent incident takes place.

Private Security at Work

Without police powers and often unarmed, what can private security officers do? Security officers cannot prevent an attack, but they can make it harder for the attacker, and lessen the damage done.

The first task is to convince top management of the need for security. To a Harvard Business School graduate or an alumnus of night school, security is not a profit center because security doesn't produce anything. This is why the security manager faces an uphill battle for funds to provide adequate security. There's no doubt that security is an overhead expense, but a necessary one.

The security manager should survey the potential target for security flaws, leaks and vulnerabilities. Private security managers have studied the differences between "soft" and "hard" targets, and know what it takes to upgrade a target to make it "hard."

A hard target has limited access, and this access is under strict control. In simple language, it's not easy to walk into a hard target, drop off a bomb, and walk away. It's not easy to walk in, burglarize desks and file cabinets, and escape undetected. It's also not easy to infiltrate a hard target by applying for employment.

Target hardening consists of a system of physical and electronic barriers, surveillance, and human protection to supplement it. Target hardening is no guarantee of protection. It just makes life more difficult for an intruder or terrorist, in the hope of persuading him to choose another, easier target.

One opinion is that the terrorist bomber will not be deterred by security measures.[2] Experience has proved otherwise. Some terrorists will, and others won't. This is why a comprehensive security program aims not only at deterring an attack, but at facilitating identification and apprehension of the perpetrators if deterrence fails.

The security manager maintains liaison with local law enforcement, firefighters, and other emergency services. In case of emergency, the security manager knows the appropriate service to call.

Security also involves checking the backgrounds of employment applicants, to screen out those with criminal histories and inferior work performances to prevent penetration by inimical elements. Security risks include members of violent radical groups, inimical or subversive political organizations, and those owing allegiance to a foreign power or even a rival business.

The Private Security Department

A continuing controversy is whether a company should set up its own in-house security department, or hire contract guards. Briefly, the arguments center around cost and competence. Hiring "rent-a-cops" is cheaper. The security forces hired are not necessarily competent, however, because of the lack of standards for private security agents. States which license security guards concentrate on checking applicants for criminal histories and establishing their proficiency with firearms (if armed). The bottom line is that any outside security personnel must owe their primary loyalty to their employer, not their client.

An in-house security department, with a security manager responsible to the CEO or his designate, is the best way to provide comprehensive security adapted to the company's needs. This isn't cheap. Hiring a former police executive, retired FBI or Secret Service agent, or private security specialist is likely to be expensive. A $50,000 annual salary isn't unreasonable for a qualified person, and higher salaries are not uncommon. Security directors of multi-national corporations make an average of over $150,000 per year, and the national average for security directors is $63,000. As with other labor costs, salaries for security personnel vary with the area.

Another function in which the security department plays a vital role is crisis management. Every company should have a crisis management team to deal with special problems such as threats, extortion, kidnapping, disasters, and other catastrophic events. Security necessarily plays an important role in such an effort, which should include top management, public relations, personnel, and plant maintenance in the basic cadre.

Access Control

One function of a private security department is controlling access to the premises. This can be as simple as having a fence to restrict access to a few gates that can be guarded, or it can include intrusion alarms over the entire area.

A fence does no good if visitors are able to penetrate it casually. A system of passes or electronic badges will ensure that only authorized personnel gain entry. Others must present identification and be "cleared" by security before admittance.

All visitors should sign in, and list the party whom they're visiting. The security guard verifies this by telephone before issuing a temporary visitor's badge. In high-security areas, all visitors should have an escort.

If bombing is a credible threat, the perimeter fence should be far enough away from buildings to reduce the effect of a truck bomb detonated outside the perimeter. All vehicles should be checked out by a guard before being admitted. The delivery gate guard should have a list of scheduled deliveries each day, and each vehicle should be checked off against the list.

To tighten security further, each driver should be checked out by the security department and issued a permanent badge to facilitate identification and allow guards to concentrate on occasional drivers without badges. If vehicle inspection is a prerequisite to admission, and it should be, guards must be armed. An unarmed guard won't have a chance of stopping a vehicle bomb, because its driver is likely to be armed.

Security guards should also conduct surveillance of the areas outside the plant, seeking anything that appears out of place. A car or truck parking in front of the building where vehicles normally don't park, for example, is cause for discreet investigation. This is especially important in case of a fire, bombing, or bomb threat, because some perpetrators enjoy observing the commotion. Discreetly photographing the crowd during a fire or bomb evacuation can provide leads, as well as evidence of the perpetrator's presence if the threat turns out to be real.

At certain well-guarded premises where threats are high, access is closely controlled. One Kansas City abortion clinic, for example, locks its front doors, and security guards check the names of women arriving for abortion appointments against a list. Another clinic has issued ballistic vests to some staffers.[3]

Other precautions to take in high-threat areas are:

Remove plants and other items where someone could hide a bomb in building lobbies and other public areas.

Eliminate open spaces above or below cabinets.

Have spring-loaded, self-locking doors on bathrooms.

Check trash baskets frequently and empty them to avoid building up trash that could conceal a bomb.

If there's reason to believe that executives are the targets, remove their names from their doors, re-assign parking spaces, and eliminate reserved parking.

Public events are vulnerable to terrorism, and private security often becomes involved to prevent unauthorized access. Security officials for Atlanta's 1996 Olympic Games, for example, will employ microchips embedded in I.D. badges to provide control of people in sensitive areas.

Establishing Surveillance

Setting up human and/or electronic surveillance of a threatened site can both deter attacks and facilitate apprehension of perpetrators. Highly visible cameras complicate the picture for attackers committing arson or planting bombs, who don't want to be identified. This is true whether the cameras are actual closed-circuit TV cameras or merely dummies. More serious attackers, such as kidnappers and shooters, are more likely to disregard surveillance.

Sophisticated terrorists know that it's possible to identify a dummy camera because it doesn't produce oscillations that can be detected by holding a small portable radio next to it. [4] This is why any dummy cameras must be located out of reach of passers-by.

Apprehension is much easier when there is a videotape record of the crime. An Albuquerque, New Mexico, man with a history of attacks on abortion clinics was arrested after he rammed a shopping cart containing a fire-bomb through the glass door of an Albuquerque abortion clinic in 1995. [5]

There have been changes on some building designs to make them more explosion-resistant. A week after the World Trade Center bombing, a major corporation changed the design of its new headquarters to include a security gate and parking away from the building, instead of basement parking.

Airline security has been inconsistent, with privately employed contract security officers screening passengers and their baggage at most airports. One off-duty police officer meeting his wife at Phoenix's Sky Harbor Airport a few years ago had a Colt Model 1911 auto pistol tucked into his belt under his jacket. He was surprised to find that he'd passed through the metal detector gate without the alarm ringing. [6]

One security procedure that shows promise is coding airfreight shipments to indicate whether they're from regular customers, or single shipments. Single shipments from occasional or one-time customers are more likely to require physical inspection.

Security procedures can be effective, but only if they're followed. Pan American Airlines allegedly did not follow a written Federal Aviation Administration rule requiring physical search of unaccompanied luggage before allowing it on board an airliner in 1990.[7]

Part of the problem is political. In 1990, the President's Commission on Aviation Security and Terrorism proposed some 60 security measures for enhancing the safety of airlines against terrorist attacks. These included questioning each passenger regarding his luggage, asking if he packed them personally, and if they'd been outside the passenger's possession since packing. Other questions would deal with reasons for the trip, whether the passenger was carrying any gifts, or whether he was carrying a package for someone else. Passengers would have to pass through a high-sensitivity metal detector that would pick up metal eyeglass frames and belt buckles, as well as coins. Each passenger would have to personally identify his luggage at the aircraft before it was loaded onto the plane. [8]

The Bush administration did not adopt the recommendations of its own commission, and the Clinton Administration hasn't either. It's unlikely, because air travelers already put up with hassles at the airport, and despite surveys saying that they would accept delays, are probably unwilling to put up with them.

Surveillance can be problematic when the area to be protected is vast, as in forests used by lumber companies. Manned surveillance is impractical. Electronic detection by motion sensors is chancy because wildlife can set off an alarm just as a human can. Tree spikers have free run.

One type of surveillance that can be effective is passing every log through a metal detector before processing at the sawmill. This will pick up metal spikes, but it's important to be aware of countermeasures used by monkeywrenchers. The most effective is using ceramic and plastic spikes, undetectable by metal detectors.[9] The only security inspection that can work against such spikes is to inspect each log visually, looking for holes. Tree spikers normally patch their holes with wood and bark, but traces of tampering may be visible, especially if they worked at night.

Employee Screening

Terrorists such as animal-rights activists and others have at times infiltrated their targets for reconnaissance in preparation for sabotage. On an individual level, mentally unstable applicants become mentally unstable employees, and are prone to workplace violence. This is why pre-employment screening is more important today than ever before. A prospective employee must not only be competent, he must not become a liability.

Employee screening must include a background check. Paper and pencil "honesty" tests simply don't cut it.[10] Another problem with "honesty" and "screening" tests is that they're illegal in Massachusetts and regulated in several other states.[11] The January, 1991, issue of *Security Management* contained a letter from a security consultant stating that a background check is superior to any paper and pencil test.

Another problem with these tests is that they're not reliable, especially because the knowledge to "beat" them is widespread. There is at least one book, and individual chapters in several other books, providing information on test rationale, construction, and vulnerabilities.[12]

Polygraph tests have similar faults, although they've been sold to businesses by an aggressive corps of testers whose livings depend on administering tests. Unwilling to admit their faults, these testers have spent decades selling their service to gullible clients, including the Central Intelligence Agency[13] and the armed services.

Background checks are critically important in verifying an applicant's past. Checking past employment records can detect those who have falsified large parts of their applications. This type of check is desirable on general personnel grounds as well as for security.

Private investigative agencies, having no official powers, must be more creative in developing information by interviewing an applicant's relatives and associates. Investigators have to employ guile, instead of coercion, to obtain information. They have developed a variety of pretext techniques for ferreting out information people might not want to disclose. On-the-spot interviews with former employers, friends, and neighbors can disclose more information. However, membership in a terrorist organization is far harder to uncover.

Private investigative agencies have a far harder time digging out illicit memberships than previous employment or criminal convictions. Although police agencies may have infiltrated terrorist organizations to obtain membership lists and other information, they don't usually share their information with private investigators.

Finding an applicant's affiliations isn't always helpful. Membership in the Friends of Animals or the Humane Society doesn't mean that the applicant is an animal-rights terrorist. Dangerous terrorist organizations don't publish membership lists or print magazines. A private investigator's resources are limited. Infiltrating a terrorist organization to find out if a certain person is a member is expensive, time-consuming, and uncertain. Rooting through an applicant's garbage is another investigative technique that works in other applications. But searching for paperwork relating to membership in a terrorist organization is likely to be unrewarding. Terrorist organizations don't issue membership cards and receipts for dues.

Background checks have their limitations, as well, although they're far better than tests. With computerized databases, a private investigative agency can run a check for criminal convictions quickly and cheaply. However, some private investigators who are former police officers use their law enforcement contacts to tap into the FBI's National Crime Information Center (NCIC) and the Interstate Identification Index (III), which is illegal. The Philadelphia Naval Shipyard Police's chief was charged on April 27, 1995, with tapping into confidential records and illegally selling them to private investigators. [14]

Intake processing of new employees should include having them fill out a lengthy application form to obtain a sample of their handwriting. Processing should also include photographing and fingerprinting, because these personal identifiers can be valuable in case of accident, termination, crank or threatening letters, or later suspicion of a crime. These should be kept on file, and both photographs and handwriting exemplars should be renewed regularly as the person ages. The personnel office should retain terminated employees' files for at least ten years after their departure.

Employee Training

Employee security training is another area where private security consultants make a difference. One important facet is handling incoming mail.

Incoming mail may include crank mail and letter or package bombs, all of which call for special handling. Mail room employees, secretaries, and others involved in the initial processing of incoming mail can be trained to recognize mail requiring special procedures.

Additional help from technology is available in the form of a letter bomb detector. The "Scanmail" 10K is a desktop scanner that measures the amount of metal, such as paperclips and staples, in incoming mail, and detects larger-than-normal amounts, which could be part of an explosive device. This is available from:

Allied Products International, Inc.
1135 Clifton Avenue
Clifton, NJ 07013
Phone: (201) 472-0757
Fax: (201) 472-6679

A crank and/or threatening letter should be handled as little as possible once the person opening the mail recognizes its nature, and preferably put inside a transparent envelope to allow reading without marring fingerprints. Preservation becomes extremely important because fingerprint processing may not take place for a long time. While sending a threatening letter is a federal crime, and postal inspectors will process the letter to trace the sender, crank mail is not a crime. However, crank letters may be precursors of more serious acts at some time in the future. The sender of a crank letter may be a harmless eccentric who eventually burns out when nobody answers his letters, but he may also be someone with a smoldering grudge that eventually explodes. A file of crank letters provides a harvest of leads when beginning the investigation of a bombing or arson.

A crank letter file provides samples of handwriting or typewriting to compare against threatening letters. The crank writer doesn't necessarily fear prosecution, and may even sign his name. The writer of a threatening letter usually knows he's open to prosecution, and may use a "handle" or not sign his letter at all.

Mail bombs are special cases, but there exists a checklist to help identify them. Suspicious items require professional handling by explosives disposal experts.[15]

A letter or package that appears to be greasy, or is leaking oily liquid, requires special handling. So does one with tinfoil or aluminum wrapping, wires, or strings through holes in the wrapping. Any package with one or more holes, or visible lumps, also requires caution.

Other tip-offs are incorrect or misspelled names, titles, or addresses, lack of a return address, or an item which is addressed to people no longer there. Remember the Unabomber?

Yet another tip-off is excessive postage, because a bomber may be reluctant to stand before a postal clerk who may remember him or her. The bomber places more than enough stamps on the package to ensure it's not held up for insufficient postage.

When mail-handlers or secretaries receive a suspicious package or envelope, they should place it in a pre-designated empty room or other secure area and call the company security officer. The security manager can make a further determination whether the package is dangerous or not, and call police if necessary.

Anyone who receives such a suspicious package at home, or who works for a company too small to have a security department, should be careful with unexpected parcels. Discretion is the better part of valor, and calling the police is better than being blown up.

If employees find a suspicious package or device on the premises, they should stay away from it and prevent anyone from tampering with it. An employee should call the security manager, who will then direct further action.

If the location of a bomb remains unknown after a bomb threat, the security manager should direct a search for it. Searchers should be predesignated, trained employees who work in the area, because they know best what belongs and what may be out of place. The search should be in a pattern, to ensure that searchers don't overlook any likely hiding place. One pattern can be to search areas above waist-level first, then proceed to lower areas. One team can search a room or area clockwise, and the other counterclockwise.

If it becomes necessary to call a police bomb team, a set of floor plans should be ready for them. These should have work and office areas clearly marked. Plans of temperature control systems and ventilation ducts should also be on hand.

Training employees to handle bomb threats is also part of the security picture. All employees with telephones should receive security training and a copy of the bomb threat checklist. See Appendix I.

It's valuable to be able to record bomb threats, because the recording can provide many more details, including the caller's voice, than a harried employee can hurriedly write on the bomb threat checklist while listening to the telephone. A recording is priceless, and recording devices should be available to switchboard operators, receptionists, and security stations, where most incoming calls will arrive. For legal reasons, it's best not to admit purposefully recording calls. A cover story is that the machine was left running "accidentally" during the call. [16]

Many telephone companies now offer a call-tracing service for a small fee. Some require only punching *57 on a touch-tone pad to start the trace. This enables a subscriber to trace threatening or harassing calls. The caller's identity is not made available to the subscriber, but goes to the telephone company security officer. Police can obtain this information for a prosecution. [17]

"Call Return" service is also available in some areas. By pressing *69, the receiver of the call can initiate an immediate call-back to the number. Informing the caller that "We know who you are" will discourage crank bomb threats. However, this has its limits, because it does not work with "blocked" numbers. Unlisted parties have blocked numbers. Anyone who presses *67 can have his number blocked for that particular call.

Building evacuation is another contingency plan. It's important to evacuate a building in an orderly way without advertising that the reason is a bomb threat. This is why a fire drill plan, rehearsed periodically, is important. This allows efficient evacuation without causing panic, because it appears to be a drill. A security guard or other trusted person should turn off gas and electricity to the building upon leaving to minimize the damage if the threat is real. [18]

Employee Termination

Another area of concern for the security manager is tracking the terminated employee. Although it's good security practice to ease terminated employees out of the plant as quickly as possible, some employers overdo the security aspect. Having an armed guard escort the employee to the parking lot and then confiscate his parking permit is heavy-handed, and causes unnecessary resentment.

Some employees will take it hard when their years of loyalty are rewarded by being casually discarded, especially if the dismissal is ignominious. A disgruntled employee may make threats against management or other employees, and may actually return to harm individuals he considers responsible for his plight or to cause physical damage. This is the type of person one security manager termed a "ticking time bomb."

One former employee in San Diego returned to the company, stalking the supervisors who had laid him off three months previously in 1991. After dispersing fire-bombs as diversions, he shotgunned the telephone switchboard. He then walked to the executive suite and shot two company officers to death. [19]

Assessing the threat from such a person requires keeping track of him after dismissal. Interviewing remaining employees who keep in touch with him helps the security manager assess his mood, and whether or not he's still talking about returning for revenge. Milking his contacts for information regarding whether the former employee still lives in the area, and whether or not he's found employment, can help the security manager decide whether or not he's a threat. If he is, it's time to retrieve his personnel files, with photographs, fingerprints, and handwriting exemplars, from the personnel office.

If the ex-employee is a threat, distributing his description and photograph to all security guards can help prevent this individual's gaining access to the plant on a pretext. Another precaution is to notify police if he's made an overt threat. If any bomb threats or threatening letters arrive, it should be routine to compare them with the files of former employees, because often this forms the first suspect list.

Public Relations

Normally, security doesn't become involved in public relations, according to the organizational chart. However, security has an important role to play because security officers come in contact with employees and the public daily.

A security department should not only be professional and competent, but should appear that way as well. Well-groomed guards who are both competent and polite make a good impression. The worst impression possible is that of unkempt, undisciplined guards with "jack-booted thugs" written all over them. Presenting a positive image requires constant effort, and one mistake can compromise many months' work.

Security has an important role in crisis management, and the security director should always be part of any crisis management team. An example is the Tylenol contamination case of 1982, when Johnson & Johnson faced what was probably the worst crisis in its history. With 20-20 hindsight, it's evident that Johnson & Johnson management handled the crisis as well as anyone could have.

Some businessmen feel that dealing with the media is futile, because they can't control the information released. Actually, stonewalling only antagonizes reporters, who will then feel free to print speculation that can damage the company's interest. J&J faced the problem squarely, admitted that their product had been contaminated, then announced the introduction of tamper-resistant packaging. J&J regained and surpassed their "market share" within 18 months. [20]

Private Intelligence Functions

Private security offers some intelligence-gathering functions, despite not having legal access to the national Crime Information Center and other restricted official sources. With computers, the gathering and organizing of information about individuals and groups is much quicker and more thorough than what was possible only a few years ago. By tapping into open sources, such as news services, the Internet, World Wide Web, and private security gateways, a private investigative or information service can develop information regarding threats in specific locales, including foreign counties, and other security information.

There are also privately run organizations, such as the Anti-Defamation League and Klanwatch, monitoring terrorist groups. Using public sources, such as news services, these organizations can locate active groups and individuals. The value of such information is limited, because these groups direct their attention more on an ideological basis than on the propensity for terrorism. Thus, an organization or individual who holds inimical views, such as one who speaks out against civil rights or against a particular ethnic minority, will be listed, regardless of whether or not this person has committed any crime.

Legal Action

The security department also has to prepare for its day in court, assisting criminal prosecution or a civil action. When guards apprehend intruders, there may be a decision to prosecute in order to deter others, even if the intruder did no damage. Security officers have to be prepared to cooperate with police and prosecutors.

Civil proceedings are also sometimes in the cards. One expert has stated that animal-rights terrorists are more likely to be deterred by civil action than criminal prosecution.[21]

Personal Protection

The bodyguard industry is also a growth industry. Corporate executives employ "executive protection specialists," or bodyguards, to ensure their safety from kidnapping and attack. One executive hired a security firm to provide miniature homing devices for his children to allow locating them in case of kidnapping.

Other security measures now employed by high-profile people who feel threatened are remote starters for personal vehicles, closed-circuit TV for their residences, motion detectors and other sophisticated alarms, "panic buttons," and bullet-resistant glass. Commuting to work at different times and by different routes makes it more difficult for a terrorist to get a fix on the protectee, and using a low-profile vehicle avoids advertising his importance.

Protective agents can advise their clients regarding other security tactics, and provide personal protection by covering the client 24 hours a day if the budget allows. It's hard to determine how serious the threat to a particular individual may be, which is why the budget is often the final determinant.

ASIS

The American Society for Industrial Security (ASIS) is this country's leading security organization. It's an association of people directly and tangentially involved in the security industry, and ASIS maintains standards of competence to which members can aspire. ASIS conducts regular seminars on security-related topics, such as terrorism, plant protection, and computer security. Security professionals may contact:

American Society for Industrial Security
1655 North Fort Myer Drive, Suite 1200
Arlington, VA 22209-3198
Phone: (703) 522-5800
Fax: (703) 243-4954

Limits of Private Security

With all that, private security goes only so far. Lacking official police powers, private security has severe limitations. Guard forces and "security checks" have their limits. A clever and determined terrorist can work his way past rent-a-cops to explore his target and formulate his attack plan. One study refers to this danger in many places.[22]

Even official law enforcement agencies cannot guarantee personal safety. Dignitaries on both sides of the Atlantic have been assassinated and kidnapped, despite the efforts of professional government bodyguards. Italian terrorists kidnapped, then killed Aldo Moro, leader of the Christian Democratic Party, in 1978, killing five bodyguards during the kidnapping.

Target hardening makes it more difficult to attack a particular structure or organization, but this merely diverts the attack elsewhere. The terrorist simply chooses an easier target, because it's not a perfect world. Private security can provide protection and peace of mind, but this is always relative.

Notes:

1. James, Frank, and McNulty, Timothy, "The Jungle Out There," *Chicago Tribune*, June 4, 1995.
2. *Counterbomb*, Myers, Lawrence W., Boulder, CO, Paladin Press, 1991, p. 29.

3. "Clinic Shooting: Planned Parenthood Says Tightened Security Alone Won't Stop Violence," Associated Press, December 31, 1994.
4. *Counterbomb*, Myers, Lawrence W., Boulder, CO, Paladin Press, 1991, p. 28.
5. Pells, Eddie, "Abortion Clinic: Man Charged in Four Instances," Associated Press, February 24, 1995.
6. The officer is a acquaintance of the author's.
7. "Hot Air, Cold Fear," *The Economist*, v315, n7655, May 19, 1990, p. 29.
8. Magnusen, Ed, "More Security, More Delays," *Time*, May 28, 1990, p. 25.
9. Foreman, Dave, and Haywood, Bill, *Ecodefense: A Field Guide to Monkeywrenching*, Second Edition, Tucson, AZ, Ned Ludd Books, 1987, pp. 44-48.
10. *Secrets of Successful Job Hunting*, Lesce, Tony, Boulder, CO, Paladin Press, 1994, p. 59.
11. Bennett, Stephen, "Employee Testing: Truth and Consequences," *Progressive Grocer*, October, 1990, p. 51.
12. *Pre-employment Integrity Testing*, Clifton, Charles, Boulder, CO, Paladin Press, 1993.
13. Aldrich Ames was one recent and spectacular failure of the polygraph. Although tested more than once, his career betraying his agency and his country spanned years.
14. *Law Enforcement News*, Vol. XXI, No. 423, May 15, 1995, p. 4.
15. "Blasting Impression," *Security Management*, May, 1995, p. 11.
16. *Counterbomb*, Myers, Lawrence W., Boulder, CO, Paladin Press, 1991, p. 11.
17. *Ibid.*, pp. 13-14.
18. *Ibid.*, p. 20.
19. "Laid-off Worker Returns, Detonates Bombs, 2 Killed", *Los Angeles Times*, June 15, 1991.

20. Withington, John, "Terror on the High Street," *Management Today*, January, 1990, p. 56.
21. Burke, Robert R., and Hall, Gwendolyn F., "The Roar Over Animal Rights," *Security Management*, v34, n9, September, 1990, p. 132.
22. *Technological Terrorism*, Clark, Richard C., Old Greenwich, CT, Devin-Adair Company, 1980, pp. 15-16, 22, 24, 31-32, and 55.

Chapter Sixteen
Self-Protection

A major theme in this book is that the government cannot protect you, and doesn't really intend to. We saw this throughout the Cold War, when the government spent billions of dollars building underground command centers for its personnel, but built no credible civil defense system because the American population was expendable.

Today, the president is as protected as anyone can be, in the White House fortress, with hundreds of federal officers to safeguard him and his family. Congress has its own police force, and every major government agency has security officers to provide a lesser degree of protection for its employees and property.

Protecting yourself against terrorism is in one sense fairly easy. Most self-protective measures and tactics are similar to those used for protection against street crime. In another sense, self-protection is very difficult because terrorism is different from street crime.

One normal and obvious self-protective measure is keeping a low profile to avoid making yourself stand out as a desirable target. Keeping a low profile is not very difficult, and the best way to demonstrate it is to show how to maintain a high profile that attracts terrorist attention:

- Direct or work for an abortion clinic.
- Join a controversial political or militant organization such as a fringe political party, homosexual group, or gun control organization.

- Join any sort of racially based organization.
- Travel to a country experiencing local disturbances, terrorism, and anti-American attacks.

Blending in with the crowd at work and in private life helps maintain a low profile. You're far less likely to be kidnapped for ransom or political concessions if you're the maintenance engineer in your company than if you're the CEO. You're far less likely to become the target of gunfire or a bomb if you remain at home than if you join a controversial public rally on abortion, homosexual rights, or a racial issue.

Be aware of happenings in your area. Keep up with the news, and don't go shopping if a controversial march or rally is scheduled in your area for that day. Also avoid political speeches or rallies of any sort. If the president, governor, or mayor plans a speech in your town, stay home and watch it on TV.

Concentrate on keeping a low profile in your daily life. Don't put bumper stickers of any sort on your vehicle. Don't dress any more expensively than is absolutely required. Avoid reserved parking spaces, even if your job entitles you to one, because a reserved space identifies you and your vehicle to any casual observer.

Maintain alertness regarding immediate events around you. Keeping an eye out for traffic hazards can also alert you to a car following you. Try to avoid narrow streets while driving, and keep an eye on conditions far ahead of your vehicle. Be alert for strangers lounging with no apparent purpose, and for vehicles that may suddenly swing out to block yours. This is good common sense, not only to avoid an ambush but to avoid the far more common traffic accident. Use the same techniques while walking. In a city, watch people around you, because you also want to avoid being annoyed by panhandlers and the occasional screwball.

You have a special advantage on home territory because you know what's normal and what's not, an advantage you lose in a strange city. You know the normal traffic density, or which vehicles are normally parked on your street. Anything out of place justifies a higher state of alertness, until you've convinced yourself that there's no danger.

At first, keeping a low profile may seem very gutless, especially if you accept the viewpoint of Dan McKinnon, formerly chairman of the Civil Aeronautics Board, who states that "...we can't let terrorists dictate where we go or when we go. If we do, they've won."[1] This applies only to people who have a stake in exposing themselves. If you're the CEO of a multinational corporation, taking risks goes with the territory. You're well-paid, and your family enjoys the benefits of your expense account, country club, travel reimbursements, stock options, and the other perks that come with the job. As an executive, your decisions affect events, and can bring you even greater rewards. You may well decide that the risks are worth taking.

On the other hand, if you're far down the totem pole, sticking your neck out is pointless. Nobody cares what you do or think as an individual, and getting caught in the line of fire is unnecessary and foolish. Yet you can be blown away by the same bomb that takes out the CEO if you're standing next to him.

Bombs and Personal Protection

Bombs are impersonal and egalitarian, although happily uncommon. In practice, there's a far greater chance of being killed in a traffic accident than by a terrorist's bomb. Still, there are some ways to protect yourself against bombs.

A routine way is to avoid areas likely to be bombed, such as airports, abortion clinics, and federal buildings. If this is impossible, spend as little time there as possible.

Receive all mail at a mail drop, both to keep your home address confidential and to keep bombs away from home during the initial delivery. At the mail drop, the clerk handling it may possibly set off a bomb intended for you. When picking up your mail, examine every piece carefully for telltale signs, and if you encounter a suspicious piece of mail, leave it alone and call police. It's far better to have the police bomb squad handle the package at the mail drop than at your home.

It's a good idea to keep your personal vehicle locked in a garage. Unprotected in a parking lot, it's a target for anyone who wants to wire a bomb to your brake pedal, or put some plastic explosive wired to a pressure switch under your seat.

If you have reason to think you're a target, give your car a once-over before getting in. Look for marks in the layer of dust around the hood and on the door handles. Open the hood and look for anything that doesn't belong. Take a peek under the chassis, and look for unfamiliar objects and stray wires.

Travel

Travel within the United States is fairly safe. Fact is, even overseas you're much more likely to be killed in a traffic accident than by a terrorist. Outside the country, travel risks can range from minimal to serious, and avoiding risks is far better policy than confronting them.

Certain locales are inherently dangerous. Visiting Germany in October and November is riskier than at other times, because of the Red Army Group's propensity for staging terrorist attacks during these months. The Middle East has been a trouble spot for years because of terrorism, wars, disease and revolutions. A simple trip to the Red Sea for a snorkeling vacation may appear harmless, but if you travel via Israel's Ben Gurion Airport, remember that although the airport is well-guarded, once you board a bus for the final leg, you're on your own. Israeli buses have been preferred bomb targets in recent years.

Another problem with the Middle East or any area where war is imminent is that you may be trapped when the shooting starts, because air carriers often stop or reroute service if they perceive a danger to their airliners. Your flight may be canceled, commandeered, or even shot down. [2]

Third World countries have risks that are far less dramatic, but no less serious, most of which are health hazards, which means that even vacations have their risks. If you visit the Grand Canyon, you'll have to contend with crowds, but visit Micronesia and you may come back with jungle rot. Each Third World country has its peculiar diseases.

It's also important to note that medical care in most Third World countries is far below American standards. Falling seriously ill becomes much more dangerous, because medical care is primitive or unavailable. A man who suffered a brain aneurysm in Haiti in 1995 was unable to obtain treatment for it in Haitian hospitals, and required evacuation to the United States. [3]

Travel insurance doesn't help much, because most policies exclude claims related to war, undeclared war, and civil war. Some travel plans specifically exclude claims resulting from terrorism, while others don't. Life insurance generally covers such claims, but don't take it for granted. It's important to check the wording of the policy and confer with the insurance carrier to be sure that the insurance covers war and terrorism. [4]

Which air carrier is safest? Obviously, avoid air carriers that have been attacked recently, or which have poor safety records. American air carriers are not as safe as French or British airlines, because of inferior safety records and a history of attacks. Airlines in the former Soviet Bloc also have poor safety records.

Avoid flights carrying military personnel, because they're natural targets. Book flights that go to your destination with as few stops as possible, because every take-off and landing is a risk. Intermediate airports may not have the same security systems as those at your origin and destination, allowing terrorists to board more easily.

Some airports have worse security arrangements than others, but experts note that none are very good. If you travel abroad, you may be impressed by the great number of flashy uniforms at one airport, but behind the facade is the simple fact that security personnel are not exactly elite troops. Terrorism expert J. Bowyer Bell went so far as to point out that those manning airport security posts are low-grade help, including "high school dropouts, senior citizens, and people holding second jobs handling security. They aren't well-trained and don't take their job seriously." [5]

For safety, avoid airline ticket offices. Some, such as El Al's, are notorious as terrorist targets, and attract both gunmen and car bombs. There's no need to visit any airline ticket office when you can buy tickets through a travel agent. Better yet, buy your tickets by phone, and mail a check for the payment.

While you can't avoid airports if you travel by air, keep your time in the airport to a minimum. Don't arrive early, and don't plan to have a meal at the airport restaurant before you depart. Instead, check your luggage early and eat at a restaurant away from the airport.

Plan your route to avoid airports that have had threats. The reason is simple. These airports will have beefed-up security, which means more delays before boarding. As we've seen, the tightest security can't prevent determined attacks at airports, and you don't want to be caught in the crossfire.

If you have to lay over between flights, don't plan to lounge in the terminal until your next flight boards. Get a hotel room away from the airport if you plan to sleep, or if time is too short, take a short walking tour of the city or have a meal in a restaurant. Today, there's another reason to eat away from airlines and airports. Airlines serve minimal food that tastes like the plastic wrapper. Airport food is of poor quality and prices are jacked up sky-high.

When you go abroad, leave your itinerary with someone you trust, with instructions to contact the U.S. State Department if you're overdue. The State Department also provides travel advisories for travelers. The number to call is (202) 647-5225.

Corporate security officials can obtain "security snapshots" of most countries in the world via computer modem. The U.S. State Department's Security Computer Network is free to any U.S. corporation doing substantial business abroad. Major American companies work with the State Department to collect and share information such as crime, travel advisories, information on terrorists, and police emergency numbers. [6]

Check your pockets, wallet and suitcase very carefully before you leave. Remove anything that might cause you problems if you're searched. You're in no position to refuse if an armed terrorist insists on examining your wallet and passport. Remove any religious symbols, as well as membership cards for a police organization, political party, or company I.D. badge. If you must have such material or sensitive documents at your destination, mail them to yourself at your hotel; don't carry them on your person.

Additional precautions for foreign travel are to dress down, instead of wearing a "power suit." Don't travel first class, because that advertises affluence. Carry luggage that doesn't stand out, instead of expensive suitcases that scream "money," and keep your U.S. passport out of sight except when you have to show it to customs officials. If you have a Rolex, leave it at home. Go to KMart and buy a Timex or Casio. They're just as accurate, but they don't advertise your affluence. Also, don't wear clothing that displays the American flag, logos of American companies, or any political slogan. Don't carry English language publications, and, of course, never carry sexually oriented magazines or alcohol when visiting a Moslem country. Anywhere you go, don't flash cash. Finally, keep your will up to date.

The key to self-protection is alertness. Remain alert when planning a trip, and when traveling. Maintain that alertness on home ground, because it can protect you from mundane threats as well as from spectacular terrorist attacks.

Notes:

1. Carroll, Doug, "How To Travel in a Troubled World," *USA Today*, October 22, 1990, p. 1E.
2. *Ibid.*
3. *Ibid.*
4. Carroll, Doug, "Insurance Provides Little Protection Against Terrorism," *USA Today*, January 29, 1991, p. 4B.
5. Cauchon, Dennis, "Strategy; Lack of Terrorism Not Surprising," *USA Today*, February 11, 1991, p. 4A.
6. Guido-O'Grady, Deborah, "Security Computer Network: Strategic Resource for U. S. Business," *U. S. Department of State Dispatch*, v1, n9, October 19, 1990, p. 227.

Chapter Seventeen
The Future

This country is wide open to terrorism. To project what the future holds, we have only to look at the past, and what is presently happening in some countries.

A rash of skyjackings during the 1960s and 1970s led to massive security measures at American airports, as well as foreign ones. Commercial airline passengers have to submit to security inspections before boarding planes or even entering the concourses leading to departure gates. They have to walk through metal detection gates, often emptying their pockets in the process. All carry-on luggage goes through an X-ray inspection, and some check-in luggage now gets similar screening.

If enough bombs detonate to whip up mass hysteria, we may expect to see the sort of generalized paranoia found today in Israel, where anyone who puts down a handbag, package or suitcase in a public place is immediately suspect. Israelis await the detonation of the next truck or bus bomb, living in anxiety because they know how terribly vulnerable they are.

Even without bombings, there are many, many airports, and all it takes to cause an atrocity is a burst of rifle fire into the cockpit when the plane is low on its landing approach.

Many people turn towards security measures to protect them. We already see metal detection gates at airports, in schools, and in many government buildings. In the future, we might find a system of passes in place at every public building and many private businesses.

It's not hard to imagine a resurgence of supermarket contamination. This time, it might not be Tylenol, but apples, pears, or anything else that is hard to place in "tamper-proof" packages. Even tamper-proof packages can be penetrated with little effort, and we might end up with battery acid in eyedrops. Fresh fruit and meats are even more vulnerable to contamination.

This is the price of living in such a complex society. Many, many parts of it are vulnerable, and nobody can do anything about it.

The situation threatens to get worse. On May 6, 1995, Iran's Foreign Minister warned of a "holy war" as a result of the United States' ban on trade with Iran.[1] The phrase "holy war" can mean almost anything, but a good possibility is terrorist strikes against United States possessions, territories and companies. A series of attacks on the U.S. mainland is certainly possible, as shown by the World Trade Center bombing.

Enter The Controllers

There has always been a controversy between those who want more government power, and those who feel that the government is already too powerful and exercises too much control over the lives of Americans. The second group points out that our civil liberties have already suffered erosion under the pretext of the "War on Drugs."

Each generation has its buzzwords and its demons, and power-seeking politicians use these stereotypes to feed their efforts for more authority. Formerly, it was "communists." Later, it became "radicals." During the last decade we've seen "drug dealers," "cults," and "militias" cited as threats to society.

The "War on Drugs" has been used as a pretext by those who want to extend government powers and control. Rationally, it's hard to see what awful threat illegal drugs pose. Both alcohol and tobacco are involved in hundreds of thousands of deaths in this country each year, far more than are attributable to illegal drugs, even if we count the homicides resulting from illegal drug traffic.

Despite massive efforts by both local and federal law enforcement officers, the amount of illegal drugs in the underground market has not decreased. However, each year has seen more involvement by the military in the "Drug War." Joint Task Force Six, based in El Paso, Texas, regularly trains local and state officers in commando tactics suitable for drug raids. Military radars are used for surveillance of airspace to find drug-carrying aircraft smuggling cargo into American territory. Today, we hear rhetoric calling for repression of free speech as well.

Soon after the Oklahoma City bombing, President Clinton and other Democrats were exploiting it in an attempt to discredit his opponents. Hysterical speeches denouncing House Speaker Newton Gingrich, radio talk show host Rush Limbaugh, and others were heard. Liberals also accused the National Rifle Association, a lobbying group, of some sort of complicity in the blast.

On a more sinister note, the president and others inside and outside of government were calling for increased police powers. This was similar to the reaction in Germany after the 1933 Reichstag Fire, when Hitler's government exploited the event to enact an array of enabling laws to repress civil liberties, political organizations, and minority groups. In both instances, those seeking more governmental power took advantage of human nature. When given a choice between freedom and security, most people will choose security, and willingly sacrifice freedom. An Associated Press poll shortly after the bombing concluded that 54 percent of those polled were ready to sacrifice "some people's" rights of privacy.[2]

Of course, sacrificing "some people's" rights is easy, but sacrificing one's own is another matter. Perhaps the wording of the questions assured those polled that they personally would remain out of the line of fire, and only "some people" would be affected.

Ever responsive to the wishes of his political masters, FBI Director Louis Freeh asked Congress for more money, personnel, and legal authority on April 27, 1995. During the same session, Freeh admitted that the FBI is "not handcuffed" in its powers of investigation of "potential domestic terrorists."[3]

This admission isn't too surprising, in the light of current FBI penetrations of homosexual groups and AIDS activists. Documents released under the Freedom of Information Act revealed that FBI informers and undercover agents attend some group meetings and report on their activities.[4]

Politics are often ruled by expediency, and political activists often switch sides when it suits their purposes. An example is Morris Seligman Dees, head of the Southern Poverty Law Center, who had asked Attorney General Reno to begin watching various "paramilitary groups" late in 1994. During the 1960s and 1970s, though, Dees advocated just the opposite. As political aide to George McGovern, Jimmy Carter, Edward Kennedy and other liberals, he sought to have government surveillance of left-wing groups decreased.

New "anti-terrorism" laws, however well-intended, will only feed the aspirations of people who want more control over our lives. If the federal government enacts a system of national identity cards, this will be merely another step towards a Big Brother establishment. Some law enforcement officials might ask for compulsory fingerprinting of all citizens, residents and visitors, in case terrorists leave their prints at the scene of a future crime. This, too, is a step towards total control, given the high-speed computers in the Automated Fingerprint Identification System (AFIS).

Stepped-up surveillance, including infiltration of various oddball organizations, is a possibility that some pundits have suggested. The FBI, of course, would be the major agency performing this surveillance. But the FBI is already infiltrating and observing various fringe groups, with no discernible benefit. FBI agents are spying on several homosexual groups, including AIDS activists, based on the "fear" that members might throw infected blood during demonstrations.[5]

Some proposed legislation has been aimed towards "terrorists." Unfortunately, when we examine these bills' provisions, we see that they affect law-abiding citizens much more than they do those who have no regard for the law.

The future will reinforce the basic fact that governments, no matter how much their officials huff and puff and demand more police powers, cannot protect their citizens against terrorism. Law enforcement officers can see that the outlook is pessimistic. Terrorism, in various forms, will probably increase, as groups concerned with political "rights," minority "rights" and even animal "rights" proliferate. As our society becomes more technological, and our systems more complex, it will be easier for extremists to disrupt and destroy them.

Notes:

1. Associated Press, May 7, 1995.
2. Goldberg, Howard, "Give U.S. Power to Protect, Most Agree," Associated Press, May 5, 1995.
3. Rankin, Robert A., "FBI Issues Warning," Knight-Ridder Newspapers, April 28, 1995.
4. Associated Press, May 16, 1995.
5. *Albuquerque Journal*, May 16, 1995.

Chapter Eighteen
For Further Reading
and Viewing

Non-fiction

Braver Men Walk Away, Peter Gurney, London, HarperCollins
Publishers, 1993. This firsthand account by a British bomb
disposal expert is fascinating reading, because during his
career, Peter Gurney disarmed a variety of bombs in
Britain and foreign countries. His insights into terrorist
bombings are a valuable guide for counterparts in this
country. Filled with good technical information, this book
is also easy reading.

Counterbomb, Lawrence W. Myers, Boulder, CO, Paladin Press,
1991. This book is a slim but practical manual on defense
against improvised explosive devices (IEDs). Several chapters cover threat assessment, building evacuation, counter-
surveillance, and active countermeasures.

Disruptive Terrorism, Victor Santoro, Port Townsend, WA,
Loompanics Unlimited, 1984. Santoro's theory is intriguing: It's possible to cause massive disruption in a society
without killing anyone. He provides many examples of
vulnerabilities that can be attacked, causing intense
disruption without lethal effects. There's enough recent
evidence to show that this can work very well, although
terrorists aren't usually sparing of human life.

Ecodefense: A Field Guide to Monkeywrenching, Edited by Dave Foreman, Tucson, AZ, Earth First! Books, 1985. This volume is a more organized anthology of monkeywrenching tricks than the original *Ecotage!* It describes how to sabotage various types of activities which environmentalists find objectionable. These are categorized as "Developments," "Roads and Tires," "Vehicles and Heavy Equipment," and "Animal Defense." The book provides instructions on how to sabotage or destroy power lines, spike trees, tamper with survey stakes, jam locks, and other disruptive techniques. The purpose is to make it expensive, dangerous, or impossible for companies environmentalists don't like to continue doing business.

While this book reads like good, clean fun, Dave Foreman and others in his organization were arrested by the FBI when they tried to sabotage power lines leading to Arizona's Palo Verde Nuclear Generating Station.

The second and enlarged 1987 edition of Dave Foreman's first book, contains 312 pp. compared to the original's 186 pp.

Ecotage! Edited by Sam Love, NY, Pocket Books, 1972. This is a collection of suggestions on how to make life hell for large corporations. Most of the suggested activities are harmless or impractical, but this book was the seminal volume for *Ecodefense*, and other volumes listing more serious techniques of sabotage.

Pre-employment Integrity Testing, Charles Clifton, Boulder, CO, Paladin Press, 1993. This is a how-to book describing ways to beat paper-and-pencil pre-employment tests. Its value to citizen and security manager alike is that it exposes the weaknesses of these oversold paper-and-pencil tests. From this book, it's easy to see why background checks are superior.

Secrets of Successful Job Hunting, Tony Lesce, Boulder, CO, Paladin Press, 1994. This book explains the dynamics of seeking employment, and the gaps in the pre-employment screening process. It's valuable reading for anyone seeking employment and any security manager trying to screen out potentially troublesome applicants.

The Silent Brotherhood, Kevin Flynn and Gary Gerhardt, NY, The Free Press, 1989. This is a detailed history of several right-wing, white supremacist and separatist organizations, most of which established headquarters in the Pacific Northwest. One of the main characters is Robert Jay Matthews, killed by FBI agents trying to apprehend him on Whidbey Island, Washington, in 1984. Another is Bruce Pierce, who had shot abrasive radio talk-show host Alan Berg to death outside his home. The main value of this book is its wealth of details, connecting one fragment of the right-wing movement to others, and the interplay with their government and left-wing adversaries.

Technological Terrorism, Richard C. Clark, Old Greenwich, CT, Devin-Adair Company, 1980. This is a somber, serious book covering the possibilities of high-tech destructiveness pitted against our society.

Terrorism, John Pynchon Holms, and Tom Burke, NY, Pinnacle Books, 1994. This is a quick treatment of the topic, very easy to read, and good for the beginner. The book contains a few technical errors, such as listing the muzzle velocity of the Ingram Model 11 9mm submachine gun as 293 fps. and the rate of fire of the Armalite AR-18 as 80 rounds per minute on full-auto. Despite these errors, this book is a compact overview of terrorism.

Terrorist Organizations in the United States, Wayman C. Mullins, Springfield, IL, Charles C. Thomas, Publisher, 1988. This book, produced by a reputable publishing firm, provides a good overview of home-grown terrorist organizations, a description of their methods, tactics and equipment, and examples of recent terrorist actions in the United States.

Fiction

Terrorist fiction is both recent and abundant, and makes very interesting reading because so much of it parallels the real world. During the height of the Cold War, the market was ripe for a rash of espionage novels and movies. Now, we've seen a surge of novels and movies with a terrorism theme. Frederick Forsyth's *Day of the Jackal* focused on France's President de Gaulle and the attempts to assassinate him. More recent books listed here deal with terrorism on American soil, and from different viewpoints. Writers such as Tom Clancy and Dale Brown are entertainers. However, William Pierce, author of *The Turner Diaries* and *Hunter*, is an ideologue, and sees the present American government as repressive and illegitimate. Authors of all stripes describe various weapons and destructive techniques with some accuracy, although not always in enough detail to allow the reader to construct his own.

The remarkable point about terrorist fiction is that much of it closely parallels real-life events. Some describe events before they happen. Dale Brown's *Storming Heaven* is a vivid recent example, describing a radio-controlled Cessna aimed at the White House. Only a few months after publication, a man piloted his Cessna towards the White House, crashing on the lawn. Walter Wager's *Otto's Boy* described a nerve gas attack on the New York subway ten years before terrorists actually did this in Tokyo.

There are two possible reasons for these close predictive parallels between life and art. One possibility is that some terrorists read these novels, and are inspired by them. There's good reason for believing this. Allen Dulles, former Director of Central Intelligence, once wrote that a special section in the C.I.A. reads all espionage novels to try to obtain workable ideas from them. It doesn't take too much imagination to see that terrorists can do exactly the same thing, because they have access to published novels as well.

The other reason is that some novelists are very bright and extremely well-informed, and develop reputations for plotting their novels with technical accuracy. Tom Clancy is one. Dale Brown is another. Both develop plots that are very plausible because they're workable and technically accurate.

This is what separates the realistic novelist from the science fiction writer. Science fiction is implausible and far-fetched. The realistic novel is very credible, and even though the events described have not yet happened, it's perfectly clear that they are possible. In some cases, they're even likely, because it's only a matter of time until someone acts upon the idea.

Attacks against the White House are a perfect textbook case. The president is such a high-profile person that attackers and copy-cats have proliferated, in some cases following each other by only a few days. His Secret Service bodyguards know it's going to be a bad day when a new attack novel appears.

Now let's take a quick look at some books and motion pictures:

All Fall Down, Lee Gruenfeld, NY, Warner Books, 1994. Lee Gruenfeld's *All Fall Down* deals with a computer nerd, in this case a female, who causes several airplane wrecks by jamming the air traffic control system and spoofing navigational aids. While the author claimed that "The events described in this book cannot happen," this merely means that the precise technique described to spoof the aircrafts' navigational instruments is unworkable. A technically capable terrorist might devise a method that works.

Debt of Honor, Tom Clancy, NY, G. P. Putnam's Sons, 1994. Like Dale Brown, Tom Clancy also visualizes an airborne attack, but on a grander scale in *Debt of Honor*. At the end of a short-term war between Japan and the United States, the captain of a Japan Air Lines 747 crashes his airliner into Washington's Capitol Building during a joint session of Congress. The crash kills the president and most congressmen, despite a last-ditch effort by a U. S. Secret Service agent who fires a Stinger missile at the approaching behemoth.

Clancy has a taste for exotic destructive devices, and earlier in his novel, a commando team causes aircraft to crash by flashing a three million candlepower light into the crew's eyes during night landings. The brilliant light dazzles and disorients both pilot and copilot during this critical stage, and the airplanes crash before the crew can regain control.

58 Minutes, Walter Wager, NY, TOR Books, 1987. *58 Minutes*, by Walter Wager, also deals with airline terrorism by similar means: jamming the airport traffic control radars, Instrument Landing Systems and radios. The author includes a disclaimer that American air traffic control systems include even more redundancies than he described in the novel, and that the sabotage as described in the book would not disable the air traffic control system.

Hunter, Andrew Macdonald (William L. Pierce), Hillsboro, WV, National Vanguard Books, 1989. This book describes the efforts of a vigilante to correct what he sees as terrible injustices in American society. It begins with his shooting a mixed-race couple, and continues with more attacks on mixed-race couples and groups. The main character moves on to assassinate a Jewish newsman, then garrotes a certain "Congressman Stephen Horowitz" who is inimical to the hero's beliefs. The hero eventually joins an underground organization that begins a revolution against the government.

Storming Heaven, Dale Brown, Berkley Books, 1994. This book depicts an attempt to crash a Cessna light plane into the White House. Perhaps by coincidence, a real-life attacker crashed a Cessna onto the south lawn of the White House a few months later. We don't know if the attacker read the book or not.

Otto's Boy, Walter Wager, NY, TOR Books, 1985. Following on the heels of real-life saboteurs, Walter Wager's "Otto's Boy" releases nerve gas in a New York City subway car in this 1985 novel of the same name. When the train arrives at 125th Street in Harlem, there are well over 100 corpses on the floor of the car. As we know, life sometimes imitates art, and Japanese terrorists recently did this in the Tokyo Subway.

Tandem Rush, Frederick Vincent Huber, NY, Dell Books, 1978. Frederick Vincent Huber's *Tandem Rush* describes how a hacker disables the telephone system. With a profusion of authentic-seeming detail, the author describes how the hacker paralyzed telephones across the country.

The plot is more complicated than that. It also includes an attempt to kill the U.S. president with a briefcase bomb on the order of the one used unsuccessfully against Adolf Hitler in 1944. Another part of the sinister plan is a van attack against the White House. Somehow, this meticulously detailed plan falls apart and the president and telephone company survive.

The Bomb That Could Lip-Read, Donald Seaman, NY, Stein and Day, 1974. This novel is almost a how-to manual, describing an Irish Republican Army splinter faction's bombing of a hotel in Northern Ireland during a high-level conference. The bomb builder uses a Bulova Accutron watch, the most advanced design of its time, to activate the bomb's listening mechanism. The detonation circuit itself uses a radio control made for model airplanes, much like the one used in a car bomb that killed *Arizona Republic* reporter Don Bolles in 1976.

The Turner Diaries, Andrew Macdonald (William L. Pierce), Arlington, VA, National Vanguard Books, 1978. The plot is an underground army struggling against a Jewish and Black controlled government during the 1990s. The "Cohen Act" bans firearms ownership and promotes integration and mixed-race sex upon whites. The underground blasts FBI headquarters in Washington, DC with a truck bomb, very much like the one used in Oklahoma City. It then engages the government in a guerrilla war, one highlight of which is Earl Turner's suicide mission of flying a 60-kiloton nuclear bomb into the Pentagon in a light aircraft. The underground eventually wins and establishes a racially pure society. The author, William Pierce, also wrote a later book under the name of "Andrew Macdonald."

The Warriors of God, William Christie, NY, St. Martin's Paperbacks, 1992. To date, there hasn't been a well-coordinated attack on the White House, only a few random shootings by unskilled individuals. This novel relates the story of an attack by Iranian agents. Unlike the irregular forces usually comprising such groups, these are hand-picked regular army troopers, landed on a North Carolina beach from a freighter. The book rolls out the preparations, the planning, and the assault, with the attackers coming very close to killing the president in the oval office.

Motion Pictures

There have also been several motion pictures dealing with terrorism. The *Die Hard* series provided good shoot-em-ups involving terrorists attacking many vulnerable targets while the intrepid police officer played by Bruce Willis frustrated their efforts.

A particularly fascinating motion picture was *Timebomb*, produced in 1984 and dealing with the attempted hijack of nuclear materials. This movie, starring Morgan Fairchild and Billy Dee Williams, depicted the nuts and bolts of transporting nuclear materials and how to hijack such a shipment. "Strategic Armored Transport" is either (the movie isn't clear about this) a company or government department charged with operating large armored trucks to make regular runs carrying nuclear materials.

Each 18-wheeler has a three-man crew, armed with handguns and M-16 rifles. The truck is armored and has a retractable turret with a .50-caliber machine-gun on top of the cab. A two-man follow-up crew, presumably armed, travels in a sedan behind the truck. Like the Department of Energy's Transportation Safeguards Division trucks, SAT's vehicles are in constant radio contact with their dispatcher.

This particular shipment is weapons-grade plutonium, and the truck leaves San Antonio, Texas, passing through Del Rio on its way to Apache Wells. A short rest stop at Del Rio allows changing drivers, while local police help guard against attack.

French-speaking Algerian terrorists ambush the truck at a 30-second radio dead spot near a power station. They fake an accident to force the truck to stop, and take out the follow-up car with a rocket launcher, while injecting gas through a rubber seal to force the truck's occupants out of the cab. The terrorists disconnect the trailer and hook it up to another tractor, while a dummy tractor-trailer continues the route to make it appear that nothing untoward had happened.

Overall, the plot appears workable. Whatever the safeguards are which exist to protect real nuclear shipments, a way exists to overcome them.

Presidential assassination is also a compelling topic for movie-makers. A classic is *Suddenly*, a 1954 motion picture starring Frank Sinatra as a psychopathic assassin. Sinatra and his gang take over a house with windows overlooking a small town train station where the president is scheduled to arrive by train and make a speech. The sniping from a window scenario described is workable, and indeed Lee Harvey Oswald did kill President Kennedy this way almost a decade later.

Appendix I
Bomb Threat Checklist

Remain calm, listen carefully, and do not interrupt or antagonize the caller. Keep the caller on the line while signaling another that you have a bomb threat working.

Date:_____

Time Received: _____

Time Call Terminated:_____

Caller's exact words: _____

Questions to Ask Caller:

When is the bomb going to explode? _____

_____

Where is the bomb right now?_____

_____

What kind of bomb is it?_____

_____

What does it look like? _____

_____

Why did you place the bomb? _____

_____

Where are you calling from?_____

_____

What is your name? _____

_____

Additional Information:

Describe caller's voice: _____

Accent: _____

Male or female: _____

Young or old:_____

Background noises: _____

_____

Appendix II
Emergency Telephone Numbers

Emergency Number: 9-1-1

Police Department: _____
Contact Person: _____

Sheriff: _____
Contact Person: _____

Level III Trauma Center: _____
Contact Person: _____

Military EOD Facility: _____
Contact Person: _____

Company CEO: _____

Contact Person: _____
Contact Person: _____
Contact Person: _____

Index

YOU WILL ALSO WANT TO READ: